D0920294

THAT'S 30!

Best wishes

Elmer Walter

THAT'S 30!

BY
ELMER D. WALTERS

TRI STAR VISUAL COMMUNICATIONS
PHOENIX, ARIZONA

ISBN: 0-9671736-0-4

Front cover credits: Rolf Sandvold, Desert Productions
Fort Mohave, AZ 86427

CONTENTS

PREFACE

An old Chinese proverb says, "To forget one's ancestors is to be a brook without a source, a tree without a root."

This book was conceived with the idea of telling future generations—my grandchildren and their grandchildren's grandchildren—of my thoughts and actions and the experiences in my life. I do not dwell at length on certain eras but on some more memorable episodes, mainly during my sailing in the U. S. Coast Guard, flying in later years, joining the U. S. Merchant Marine during the Persian Gulf War, and travels in retirement.

Some men only dream, while others make their dreams come true.

Commercial wireless radio stations would send PRESS (newsworthy items) to ships at sea. Ships would subscribe to this service to keep their passengers informed on current events. At the end of the news transmission, the radio operator would sign off with "That's 30," meaning "That's the end."

In other words, this is my story and "that's 30."

I would like to thank the following persons, who were instrumental in assisting and advising me in the writing of this book.

First, my wife, Joyce, who encouraged me nonstop to write, who tolerated the hours and hours of my ignoring her as I tried to concentrate and write, and who offered suggestions and critiques throughout the process, for her patience and support.

Helen Mosbrook, whom I was fortunate in meeting, for her able and professional editing.

Herb ("Johnny") Johnson, my Coast Guard buddy since 1950 who refreshed my memories of almost 50 years.

Maj. Bill Jakes, retired U.S. Army, who refreshed my short-term memories of Space-A travel and graciously encouraged my efforts overall.

Marjorie Barr Pratt, author of *Recollections of a Homesteader's Daughter,* who inspired me to write these memoirs.

And Bill Hines, Helen's husband, an accomplished professional pilot who assisted in defining technical terms related to flying and soaring.

That's 30!

Elmer Walters
April 1999

Instantly likeable, Elmer Walters quickly conveys to his readers the depth and range of his experiences. *That's 30!* was originally conceived as a memoir for his grandchildren. Fortunately for the rest of us, the memoirs became vignettes, and the vignettes became a breezy book with poignant human interest. His wit and self-effacing nature are portrayed throughout this work, which is easy reading and fast-moving. One cannot help but admire and respect the life of this American, who makes you feel good and enjoy the experiences along the way.

William Jakes, Major, U.S. Army, Ret.

Travel with Elmer Walters and you will experience warm camaraderie, fascinating conversations, and genuine friendship. An accomplished raconteur, in his book Elmer takes you on a trip through his "Huck Finn" youthful years (which even include a ride on a river raft), his adult years of varied and multifaceted careers and avocations, and, most recently, his adventuresome years of retirement. Elmer is one-of-a-kind, a gentleman of many talents, a man for all seasons. As you take this trip with him, you'll find yourself caught up in the fun and intrigue of it all and will enjoy every moment. You may even wish to repeat the trip, as I did. It's a winner.

John Robson, Captain, U.S. Navy, Ret.

From growing up in the '30s in upstate New York through serving in the Merchant Marine during the aftermath of the Persian Gulf War, Elmer cajoles the reader from one memory to another in this often poignant autobiography. Reminisce with him as he retraces the choices he made when opportunity knocked. We can all learn a lesson from reading what results when an adventuresome spirit is coupled with a "Can do!" attitude. *That's 30!* is definitely a "must read!"

James Sullivan

I. BIRTH

I was born at home, 27 Smith Street, Hilton, New York at 11 a.m. on Saturday, May 18, 1929. I weighed a little over 9 pounds. I was the youngest of five children of Samuel (Jr.) and Pauline (Skinner) Walters. Mrs. Sarah Dornan, a family friend, assisted in the delivery. The birth certificate was filled out three days later by Mrs. Thomas Stothard, the local registrar, at Hilton, District 2723, Req. No. 7.

According to my older sister, Jean, I went without a name for five or six days until Mother and Dad settled on Elmer DeWitt. Elmer came from my father's cousin's husband and DeWitt from my maternal grandfather, DeWitt Clinton Skinner.

I have been known for most of my life as "Tony" or "Walt." Almost everyone in Hilton knew me as Tony. All through my school days, I was known only as Tony to my schoolmates, and even now local people refer to that name. In the service, I was called Walt, and others, for years afterward, called me by that name. Sometimes it's confusing—not to me, but to others—to hear both nicknames simultaneously. Some people demand to know what my real name is, and when I tell them, they are even more confused.

1929: That's me in the buggy, being pushed by my big sister Jean. In the left foreground is Harvey, with Bob behind him. Virginia is on the right.

1

Times were good in early 1929. Mother had a part-time maid, Fanny, who would come on different days of the week. I don't remember Fanny at all because the Depression hit five months later, in October 1929, and the bottom fell out of everything.

My earliest recollection is from 1933, when I was four years old. Jean was attending Brockport Normal School (later Brockport State, University of New York), and Bob, my older brother, had graduated from Hilton High School and was taking a postgraduate course because he was only 16 and unable to find a job. Harvey, my younger brother, was 9, and Virginia, my younger sister, was 7. I was my mother's "baby," and she would jokingly call me that in public when I was as old as 35.

I am a half-brother to Jean and Robert because Mother was married before my father to an Elbert Johnston, in 1913 and he died of the "flu epidemic," in 1919.

I remember Harvey and Virginia going away early in the morning and returning home late in the afternoon. I wondered where they had gone. Later I found out the place was called "school."

1915: Family of Samuel Walters Sr. shown at the old homestead west of Wisconsin Rapids. Standing from left to right in the rear are James, Samuel Jr. (my father), Samuel Sr., John, Mother Rose, sister Rose, and Edward. In the front are Theodore and George. Three older siblings had already left home.

1905: My mother's family in Rochester, N.Y. In front, left to right, are DeWitt C. Skinner, my grandfather, his youngest daughter Beulah, and his wife Estelle (*née* Cram, my grandmother). Standing in the rear are Mildred Pauline (my mother, at age 16), Marie, and Walter.

II. CHILDREN AND FAMILY

My father, who was born and raised in Wisconsin, had met my mother in the early '20s when he came to live in Hilton. He had done farm work around Wisconsin Rapids and left to visit his eldest sister Anna in Riverside, California. While there, he made friends in Hollywood, including William S. Hart, an early cowboy silent-film star.

Dad traveled on down through San Antonio, Texas and finally ended up in Spencerport, New York, where he worked on the Kenyon family farm on the corner of North Union Street and Big Ridge Road. While working there, he met Mother, who lived on South Avenue in Hilton.

Dad was born on November 24, 1899 in Rudolph, Wisconsin. His parents were Samuel and Rose (Mathis) Walters. He was the fourth of 10 children: Perry, Anna, Joseph, Samuel Jr., Rose, James, John, Edward, Theodore, and George. Most of them lived in Wisconsin, but some migrated to California and Illinois.

Over many years of visiting my uncles, Ed and Joe in Wisconsin and John and George in California, I have come to know them and their families quite well. I met Jim in 1942, and he was a happy-go-lucky, carefree person. Ted and I met in 1946 after he was discharged from the Army; he was a more serious man and a loner. He never married but kept to himself for the rest of his life up on Big Bear Mountain, California. The others I got to know much better, along with their families. They all seemed happy and content. My cousins loved their fathers, and my uncles loved their children all through their lives. They spoke highly of one another even though they all went through rough times and never had much money.

My mother was born in Rochester, New York on July 6, 1889, the first of four children of DeWitt Clinton and Estelle Skinner. After her came Marie, Walter, and Beulah. All of them seemed to be more serious and reserved but still a loving family. All my cousins are friendly and loving, and we all have a great rapport. We all still try to get together twice a year, although some live thousands of miles away.

It was years before I realized that things were different at our house. There was no love in our family. There was no hugging, no kissing, no touching, no kind words, and no encouragement. Self-esteem was broken down—there was none!

When you're young, you don't know the difference. You think all families are like yours.

My brothers, sisters, and I were abused physically and mentally. With Dad, it was, "Shut up and be quiet!" Problems were settled with slaps, and eventually, closed fists. As the youngest, I was not treated as harshly as the other four. For the most part I seemed to escape Dad's wrath, but not always.

A case in point: I was about 7 or 8 years old, sitting at the kitchen table on a high stool, eating breakfast. My father was sitting to my left. Maybe everyone else had finished, because there was just the two of us. Maybe I was rebelling at finishing my meal—I don't remember.

Something I evidently said or did was enough to anger my dad. He leaped forward, swinging with his fist, and hit me on the left side of the face, knocking me and the stool flying. I barely remember getting up. Whether I finished breakfast I do not recall.

In this case, as always, when one of us was punished or beaten, we were left alone to lick our own wounds.

Mother, whom I loved dearly, simply turned her back and showed no love and very little compassion. What good would it do? She would feel Dad's wrath too.

I do not recall ever being encouraged to do things that kids might want to do. Our parents' relationship with the five of us was, to say the least, rarely compassionate and seldom sympathetic. We were given orders, never choices. There was seldom any appreciation for our achievements, and we were merely tolerated in the household.

November 1934: The Walters family—left to right on the sofa, my older sister Jean, my father, my mother, and my older brother Bob; seated in front, my brother Harvey, my sister Virginia, and me.

EARLY YEARS

My father had some weird ideas about religion. Harvey, Virginia, and I were raised as Catholics because Dad was a strict Catholic. We had to sit up straight in church and not make a sound; if we did, we were beaten when we got home.

Mother, a Baptist, had a Bible, but it was out of sight. The Catholic Catechism and the prayer books were the only religious books that Dad thought were to be used by laymen. All hell broke loose if we ever mentioned going to church with Mother, even on a special day like Easter Sunday, after going to Mass first.

Dad reprimanded me many times, and probably Harvey and Virginia too, for asking questions that might pertain to Biblical passages we had heard. He said it was wrong to associate too closely with Protestants, and it was a grievous, mortal sin if you dated a non-Catholic. Why? He had even married one.

Profanity was a common all-day, every-day language for Dad. For unknown reasons, he was an unhappy, angry man.

All that turmoil created problems as we children were growing up. Harvey and Virginia seemed more mature and could see right from wrong at an earlier age than I. I guess I just tolerated more abuse and said nothing.

Although Dad didn't drink (I'm sure one beer would have made him drunk), he never lacked for tobacco all his life. He smoked Union Leader, a pipe tobacco; Chesterfield cigarettes; and an occasional cigar on Sundays. All through the Depression, he made sure he had tobacco.

Mother put up with quite a bit from him. She tried to correct his manners, but "he was in charge and he wasn't going to be told" what to do.

As far back as I can remember, we had a white tablecloth and white linen napkins. We each had our own napkin ring, all of which were silver, except mine, which was plastic. We used Wm. Rogers Bros. silverplated flatware at every meal.

Jean taught all of us younger kids more manners and etiquette than anyone else. To this day I am indebted to her for all she did.

My sisters and brothers could probably write volumes on our family life.

TOYS

I have no recollection of any toys I might have had before age 4 or 5. Most of my toys after that were hand-me-downs from my older brothers, except for a few new ones I might have been given at Christmas. I don't remember any new toys until I was 6 or 7. Certainly, in those days, boys did not play with dolls. It was not considered masculine to do such a thing. Something would have been thought wrong with any boy who did.

One Christmas, when I was 6 or 7, I wanted a new fire truck because the one I had had been given to one of my brothers 10 years before. I wrote a letter to Santa Claus asking him for a new fire truck. I even left the note with a plate of cookies, to "butter him up," I guess.

On Christmas morning, I rushed downstairs, but there was no fire truck. Then I looked out on the front porch—still no truck! But I did find a crumpled piece of paper blowing in the snow on the porch. It was my letter to Santa, and he had taken the cookies, plate and all.

That was when I found out there was no Santa Claus (sorry, Virginia O'Hanlon*). Harvey and my sister Virginia had been telling me for two years that there was no Santa, but I refused to accept it. That episode convinced me.

HOLIDAYS

The holiday season was a time for visiting Mother's side of the family, because all of Dad's family were in Wisconsin or California. On New Year's Day we all piled into a Model A Ford and went to visit Mother's brother, Uncle Walt, and his wife, Aunt Alice. My cousins were Gordon, Roger, and Betty Skinner. They were all much older than I, about the ages of Bob and Jean. I remember that there were squirrels in the Skinners' backyard, which I thought was pretty neat because we didn't have squirrels in the village where our family lived. They would scamper across the yard and up into the trees.

There were always games to play in the Skinners' basement. Uncle Walt taught photography at Edison Technical High School. Over the years I've met friends who were in his class.

At Christmas, before we left home, we would open our presents in the morning and try to eat some breakfast with all the excitement in between. With Dad driving, Mother and I in the front, and the rest of the kids bundled up under a buffalo robe in the back, we would visit Aunt Marie and Uncle Dave Davidson. Marie was Mother's younger sister. The Davidsons had two children, Carol, who was Jean's age, and Norman (called Bud), who was Harvey's age.

---

* The Virginia of "Yes, Virginia" fame; as an 8-year-old on the edge of disbelief in 1897, she sought reassurance in a letter to the *New York Sun;* "Yes, Virginia, there is a Santa Claus," came the reply in Francis Pharcellus Church's immortal editorial: "He exists as certainly as love and generosity and devotion exist..." First published in the *Sun* on Sept. 21, 1897, it was reprinted annually before Christmas through 1949.

RELATIVES

What I remember most about the Davidsons was that my cousin Bud had the biggest electric train I'd ever seen. Each car had to be a foot long and 6 inches high. Their Christmas tree seemed to be 50 feet high. Everything at their place was always larger in the wonderment of a small boy's eyes.

Thanksgiving was usually the day we entertained the rest of Mother's relatives. We kids usually played outside in the snow most of the time because our house was small and we never had enough chairs.

Mother always prompted us younger kids to exclaim about having real butter on that day. We always had margarine every day during the rest of the year. My job was to take a 1-pound container of lard, sprinkle an orange powder on it, mix it, then form a brick and serve it on the table. There seemed to be a stigma attached to people who ate margarine because they could not afford real butter. I'm not so sure we weren't healthier through those years because of it.

I don't recall that we went to Aunt Beulah Newton's house for a holiday at any time. She was Mother's younger sister, and Uncle Port (short for Portice) was her husband. Shirley, Don, and Howard Newton were my cousins. Howard and I were about the same age; all the other cousins were older.

Grandpa Skinner used to come to visit us in later years, around 1941 to 1947. He would usually stay for three days. He drove a Model B Ford, and with the wind at his back and going downhill, he would attain maybe 30 miles per hour.

Looking back now, I suspect the car would have gone faster, but Grandpa was Grandpa. Another thing was that most people didn't drive much over 40 to 45 mph up to the early '50s. Actually the speed limit was 35 mph during the war years. After World War II, higher performance cars came on the market along with higher performance tires, oil, and gasolines.

SCHOOL

I entered school when I was 5 years old in September 1934, at Hilton School at West Avenue and Henry Street. Miss Wheaton was my first-grade teacher; she later left to marry Cornelius Vanderbeck's son.

There was no kindergarten in those days; we started in cold turkey, the very first day, learning the alphabet and numbers. It was quite a strange world, spending all day with 20 or so kids you never saw before, whereas kindergarten is a much more relaxed scene in your first year.

The second and third grades were taught by Miss Celia Burke of Hamlin in the same classroom. She was a very kind and pleasant lady. She never married, and I believe she was still teaching through the years my own children were passing through her grade.

The fourth and fifth grades were taught by Mrs. Butcher, also in the same classroom. She was quite elderly and rather stern-looking, but she was a pleasant teacher.

A few years later, Mrs. Butcher's father-in-law, Charlie Butcher, who was an old man then, lived up the street from where I lived in Hilton. For some reason he never liked me. All I did was cut cross-lots past his property, which he only rented, and he would berate me all the time.

About that same time, George Blossom was riding his bicycle cross-lots through the same property with Zeke Kelley riding crossbars. George did not see the clothesline as he rode through there, and it caught him right across the Adam's apple and took him right off his bike.

George landed flat on his back, and Zeke went sailing along on the cross bars down the street. Zeke turned around to see George on the ground, and he ended up crossing the street and tearing into a neighbor's hedge, where he came to a halt.

One day in Mrs. Butcher's fourth-grade class, we all had to read aloud an essay that we were supposed to have prepared the night before. Guess what? I had completely forgotten to write mine.

Being a very quiet and shy person, I was always called upon to recite. A few students went up front, one at a time, and read their essays.

Sure enough, I was called to come up front and read my essay. Nonchalantly, I opened my loose-leaf notebook and took out a *blank* sheet of paper. I strode to the front without hesitating and held the paper at an angle so Mrs. Butcher could not see from where she was sitting at her desk.

I proceeded to speak on the subject "The Netherlands." Having previously read my geography book, which I always found interesting, I began to talk about how the people dressed, how they would skate on the canals in the wintertime, how they farmed, raised tulips, and how the windmills worked. I dug myself into a hole at that point and couldn't think of anything more to say.

Mrs. Butcher asked, "What's the matter, Elmer? Are you stuck on a word?"

"Yes," I replied apprehensively.

"Well, bring your paper here to me and I'll help you," she said.

Nervously, I took the paper to her. She took one look at the blank sheet of paper, then looked at the other side.

The embarrassing part was having my paper shown to the class, but I don't think they truly grasped what had happened. None of them ever said anything or kidded me about it.

I think Mrs. Butcher was impressed by my standing up front, "ad-libbing" for five minutes on a subject I knew. She gave me a passing mark on my dissertation, even though she couldn't mark it down on that blank sheet.

In June 1938, I had an ear infection such that a mastoid operation was necessary on my right ear. It was quite serious in those days, before the miracle of penicillin. My mother and brother Bob rushed me to Highland Hospital in Rochester. A priest administered the last rites of the Catholic Church that evening. The doctors operated that night, but it was not successful, so they operated again the next day, behind my right ear. Everything was okay, and after a month in the hospital, I went home.

Less than two months later I went back to the same hospital for a tonsillectomy and adenoids operation. It was thought in those days that swollen tonsils were the cause of sore throats and earaches. That certainly seemed to be true in my case.

The fifth grade was taught mostly by a new teacher, Miss Betty Wedel, assisted by Mrs. Butcher. Miss Wedel was a very good teacher, and everyone liked her. Mrs. Butcher wore long, dark dresses. She was very stout, and she wore her hair done up in a bun. That was the old style. Miss Wedel was young and could identify better with the young children.

In the sixth grade we were taught by Mrs. Avis Blair, who was known to be very strict. She was that, but she was also very fair, and we kids had a lot of fun. She started the day with the Lord's Prayer, then checked for clean handkerchiefs and fingernails. She would kid around at times, but when you had homework to do, you had better have it done. Every night you could count on having arithmetic, geography, and spelling to do.

Mrs. Blair cared for her kids. She wanted us to pass, but more important, she wanted us to know the material. She loved us, and I think that almost everyone who studied under her would say that they loved her, too.

Halloween 1938 was a night to remember, not only for me but for a few million other people. Anyone who happened to tune the radio to a certain station that carried one of the network programs would hear Orson Welles's production of *The War of the Worlds*. It was very scary and sounded quite authentic, about Martians invading the Earth. People who heard it were so scared, they ran out of their homes and jumped into their cars, and some smashed them up. They would try to escape from New York City and New Jersey, where the Martian landings were supposed to have occurred. Some people even committed suicide by jumping out of windows from tall buildings.

This neighbor of my Aunt Beulah and Uncle Port, whom we happened to be visiting, came bursting into the house. She was upset, crying, and visibly shaking because she had tuned into the middle of the program.

My cousin and I had just come in from Halloweening, and our parents were trying to calm the neighbor. Uncle Port said, "It was probably some radio drama. Just stay calm and we'll see what happens for a while."

Turning the radio on, we found out shortly that as the program ended, it was a hoax.

Legislation came out later from the FCC stating that all stations and programs had to clearly identify themselves to all listeners.

One of the records in my collection includes that 1938 radio program, which I treasure.

Halloween was fun when I was little. Sometimes Mother would have cider and doughnuts for anyone who came to the door. Sometimes I went to someone's house for a party, and they invariably had cider and doughnuts or cupcakes. We played games like Pin the Tail on the Donkey and Dunking for Apples.

As we grew older, we would ring doorbells and soap windows. One storefront in the village really caught "holy-you-know-what" because the druggist was known for being cheap. He justified his reputation later, when I had a paper route.

1939

In 1939 I was in the sixth grade. My older brother Bob bought a springer spaniel from Bernie Rood, the milkman. We called him Lucky. As a hunter, he was a natural, very alert and quick to learn but also a house dog. When I was in high school during the war years, Lucky and I hunted pheasant and rabbits with my high school history teacher, Len Wright. Len was our class advisor and baseball coach; he also drove the school bus along with teaching history and civics.

Lucky was my best friend, although he was devoted to Mother because she took care of him most of the time.

During the winter of 1940-41, I seemed to have a lot of sickness. Harvey contracted scarlet fever in March 1941, and Virginia and I were quarantined for a month, so we were out of school. Then I came down with the disease, but my case was not as serious as Harvey's. He was left so weak that he had to walk with a cane for a few weeks. Jean was married by that time, and Bob had been drafted into the Army and reported to Fort Niagara.

February 1941: My dog Lucky snapped outside our house.

In June I failed seventh grade, which was quite a blow to me, but I happened to be the youngest in the class, so I joined the next class of students who were closer to my age. This was all explained to Mother by the teachers, and it made me feel a little bit better. I had been struggling a little bit, but after that it was a "piece of cake"; not that it was easy, but the pressure seemed to be much less.

Harvey tried to join the Navy in November but was rejected because he had a "heart murmur" and the Navy was quite strict. However, Dec. 7 (Pearl Harbor) happened, and things changed. Harvey walked into the Marine Corps Recruiting Office in Buffalo, N.Y., and they sent him directly from there to Parris Island, S.C. Boot Camp.

Bob served in Africa and later in southern France from 1942 to 1945 with Gen. Patch's 7th Army and ended up in Germany at the end of the war. Harvey, as a Marine, served in the eastern states guarding documents while traveling between military posts. He also guarded prisoners of war at Portsmouth, NH for the first couple of years. Then he was in the invasion of Guam and while there, he ran into two of our cousins,

Don Newton (Army) and Bud Davidson (Air Force). What a coincidence!

World War II was still going on for two more years when I was a freshman and sophomore in high school. We kids were encouraged to buy savings bonds or stamps until we accumulated a total of $18.75, the total cost of a bond, which in 10 years would mature to a value of $25.

During the war, the government set up a listening post outside our village that was manned by men, women, and some older teens who volunteered for 2- to 4-hour watches. When an airplane approached, they would call a Civil Defense number, giving information on the type of plane (if known), direction it was heading, and the estimated altitude.

There were not too many airplanes flying in our area in those days, so most people would stop to look up and watch if there was one in the area. It seemed they were mostly the Navy V-12 students learning to fly in the PT-17 Stearmans.

Sometime in 1939, my father decided that I was going to be an altar boy at St. Leo's Catholic Church. For years it had been a custom in our family that the oldest boy served in the church. For some reason, Harvey had never been an altar boy, so it was decided that I was definitely going to serve.

Serving at Mass on Sunday mornings was only part of the job. Special Masses during the week were said in the evenings or sometimes in the early morning. That meant getting up at 6 or 6:30 a.m. for a 7 a.m. Mass, then going to school. Forty hours of Devotion or Lenten services demanded more of a young boy's time.

Usually there were two of us boys who served at each Mass. We wore black cossacks, buttoned down from the neck to the ankles, with white, loose-fitting blouses on top.

At the beginning of the Mass, the other boy and I would follow the priest to the altar. The priest would recite in Latin, and the two of us (sometimes only one) would answer the chants in Latin. I still remember some of it, verbatim.

Until the reign of Pope John XXXIII in the early '60s, the Mass was said by the priest and the altar boys with their backs to the parishioners.

That never made sense to me. Pope John revolutionized the Church in many ways, and it was all for the better.

Our church over the years had some very good priests and others not so good. Father Predmore, who baptized me, was very highly esteemed. Father Davis then became a top priest in the Rochester Diocese. Father Hoar was a "real Joe," just like Bing Crosby in *Going My Way*. I don't remember whether he could sing, but he had a great rapport with us kids. He even came to the summer carnival and rode on the ferris wheel with us.

Father Burley was a priest of another sort. He would yell and scream and beat on the pulpit every Sunday, and once he flailed his arms around and swept the Bible off the lectern onto the floor. He would get beet red in the face and swear and curse us parishioners and tell us that we were all bad sinners and we were all going to hell. Everyone was afraid to cough or make any noise. We all just sat there in dead silence throughout the entire Mass.

As a kid, I was taught to "shut up and listen," but I felt that was the wrong approach, even so.

I think Father Burley was recalled by the bishop after a few months, but where he went or what happened to him, I don't know.

When I was in high school, after I had been an altar boy, we teenagers were released from school an hour early on Wednesday afternoons to attend religious instructions. We had to walk to the church for the training in the church basement.

Father Patrick O'Rourke, an old man in his 70s, taught us kids. He had one of the best personalities of anyone I remember who was "a man of the cloth." We called him "Pappy," but it was with reverence, and he knew it. He was from Our Mother of Sorrows Church, 10 miles from Hilton.

In 1998, Joyce and I attended a wedding at that church. I found Father O'Rourke's gravesite in the churchyard and told Joyce what a saint he was.

In the fall of 1940 was the Presidential election between Pres. Franklin D. Roosevelt, a Democrat, and Wendell Willkie, the Republican candidate. The politicians of Parma-Hilton had a Republican campaign headquarters office on Main Street, and on election night they would pass out cigars to all Republicans, including my dad, and the women and kids were given candy. We kids got 5-cent Milky Way bars; quite a treat. I also got a large poster from the Democrats' campaign headquarters office. I forget where it was, but the poster depicted FDR and his New Deal. I still have it today.

The old-time politicians in the area were quite impressive in those days, with their pot-bellies bursting out of their suits with vests and their big cigars stuck in their mouths. Unhappily, though, for the local Republicans, they were not on the winning side, because Roosevelt won an unprecedented third term.

At that stage in my life, I loved reading adventure stories, such as *Ivanhoe, Kidnapped, Treasure Island* by Robert Louis Stevenson, *Lafayette Escadrille* by Nordhoff and Hall, and "Tom Swift" books like *Tom Swift & the Caves of Ice.* Yes, I did read my share of "Superman," "The Flame," and later "Batman & Robin" comic books.

I loved sports, especially baseball. My favorite teams were the Rochester Red Wings and the New York Yankees. For years I knew all the players on both teams. I followed them every day in the sports pages of the newspaper, right after the comics.

One of the problems of the Red Wings was that as soon as one player did well, their parent club, the St. Louis Cardinals, would call up that player to the major leagues. I noticed time and time again that the Cardinals would make the player sit on the bench and not play, then eventually sell or trade him. That was why I disliked the Cardinal organization, but they had good teams nevertheless.

Later in the '50s the Cardinals decided to drop the Red Wings, and the Baltimore Orioles picked up the Rochester club. Over the years I looked forward to seeing a few games when I was in town.

GAMES

The Barefoot Boy

Blessings on thee, little man,
Barefoot boy with cheek of tan!...
Ah! that thou couldst know thy joy,
Ere it passes, barefoot boy!

—*John Greenleaf Whittier*

When I was about 10 to 15 years old, we kids would go to the "ol' swimmin' hole" on Salmon Creek, south of the West Avenue school and in back of the school baseball diamond in Hilton. At that time, there was no school there, of course; it was all farmland, and in our young eyes it was worlds away from civilization. There we would have fun in the summer. One of the most famous aquatic performances was called "pickle on the platter," and there was the usual "mooning" demonstration.

The bank was wet clay and slippery, so you either jumped in or fell in. You couldn't get enough of a toe grip to dive.

One of the guys stood on the bank in all his "birthday splendor" and "shook the lily" at the farmer's wife when she happened to drive by in her car on the dirt lane. We laughed 'til we cried, and to this day I'm sure he couldn't remember why he did it.

After swimming, we would play on Lee's Hill, the high embankment along the south side of the creek on the way back to the real world in the village. Along there we passed through a sour cherry orchard, and I believe there were some sweet cherry trees, too. We usually had our fill of fruit for the day, and it often kept us regular. My dog, Lucky, a springer and water spaniel mix, would be with me almost all the time when we were out playing. Sometimes he would be off hunting or sniffing rabbits or pheasants by himself, but he always showed up when we left to go home.

Once my friend Jim and I had a log raft made from 4-inch fence posts (actually another kid made it). We packed a lunch, and the two of us, with Lucky, sailed on down the creek from Hilton to Braddock Bay, an outlet onto Lake Ontario, maybe a two- to three-mile trip. The three of us had a ball, and that was the start of my love for the sea. To this day, no sailing on the oceans was any greater than that day drifting down Salmon Creek.

On the raft, we had an orange crate where we placed our lunches and bottles of Kool Aid. The raft was hidden in a secluded inlet and covered with tree branches.

Lucky loved the water, so he was raring to go. Jim and I each had a pole for controlling the raft. We all hopped aboard and poled out to the middle of the stream.

The first landmark was an old brick chimney about 60 to 70 feet tall, all that remained from an apple-drying house that had been destroyed by a fire long ago, I had heard. Drifting, we passed the Hilton Milling & Warehouse Co., where telephone poles were stacked and stored near the bank before being used by the Rochester Gas & Electric Co.

Shortly, we sailed by the cold storage where two men who worked at the power plant were lounging in the noonday sun. They waved and greeted us.

"Wally!" Seegar yelled out. "Where're you headed, boys?"

"To Braddock Bay!" we answered. It wasn't far, but in our minds it might as well have been Cape Cod.

Ed Kleinback, who was sitting in an old chair propped up against the building, asked jokingly, "Have you got room for me too?"

"Sure, hop aboard!" Jim yelled as we cruised on by.

Lucky, busily observing the fellows on land, was excited and wagged his tail a mile a minute.

The water got a little deeper at that point, and soon we turned as the creek made a sharp left bend to the north. About 200 yards ahead was the railroad trestle, and at that moment one of the two daily freight trains was passing over.

It was usually a short train, with a steam locomotive, its coal tender, and eight or ten freight cars. This was known as the "Hojack Line," a branch of the New York Central, which was the Niagara Falls, Rome, Utica, and Ogdensburg trunk.

As the train approached the village to the west, we continued under the trestle, and directly on the right was the "hobo jungle," an old railroad watering and coaling station alongside the track. Only the cement foundation was left.

In those days, hoboes were occasionally known to come into the village and work for food. Hoboes are not bums; bums beg for food and are too lazy to work. More than once, when I was little, a hobo would knock on our back door and ask for something to do—for a meal. They might sharpen knives or clean windows. After their work, Mother would have them sit out on the back steps and eat the dinner she had prepared for them.

One day when I was 8 or 9, after attending Sunday Mass, my father asked me if I wanted to go on a hike. We went down to the tracks and headed out toward the railroad trestle, carrying a paper bag. Dad had potatoes and a loaf of bread in the bag, and we walked over the trestle to the "hobo jungle" to give Old Tom, the hobo, some food.

Old Tom was a familiar face to many folks in town. The top half of his left ear had been eaten off by something or someone. He wouldn't hurt a fly, and on that Sunday morning he was cooking (snapping) turtle soup. He was grateful for the spuds and bread to add to his turtle soup dinner.

Sailing past the "jungle," we came upon some shallow areas where the water barely carried us over the stones. The creek twisted and turned until we passed under the Wilder Road Bridge, which led into the village.

The final mile was fairly straight and deep, and we were careful not to "rock the boat." Approaching Black's Woods, we kept looking for the old Boy Scout camp and cabin that were near the bank. When we found it, we pulled over to the side and decided to put our spare shirts and lunches up in the crotch of a tree about 10 or 12 feet from the ground. Then we went on downstream to the outlet of the creek to Braddock Bay. There we tied up near a little restaurant, where we bought a couple of candy bars.

Poling our way upstream, we arrived at the camp where we had stashed our stuff, only to find that some man had pitched a tent and was fishing right at our landing site. We went ashore to get the gear we had put up in the tree only a couple of hours earlier. The man was completely surprised that he had not seen our stuff right above his head. Jim and I laughed about that, and the fellow did, too.

THE VILLAGE SMITHY

"Under the spreading chestnut tree, the village smithy stands" on Railroad Avenue in Hilton, at least until the late '30s or early '40s.

Offering me some of those little red hot cinnamon candies, Harvey said, "Here, take some. They're kind of hot, though."

"Where did you get the candy?" I asked.

"Over at the blacksmith shop," replied Harvey. He and his best friend, Joe Kelley, would go over to the shop and watch Julian Perry, the village blacksmith. Some of my friends and I would go there on occasion, too, but I don't remember Mr. Perry ever giving any candy to us.

There were still quite a few horses around town that needed to be shod, and some days there might be two or three wagons in line. Each farmer would unhitch one of his horses and lead it inside the shop with the reins. The shop had a smell all its own, and the walls and ceiling were darkened from a coal or coke fire pot that always had red hot embers in it. The ceiling beams were oak or ash, with 12- to 14-inch sides, and must have weighed hundreds of pounds. They were blackened by the smoke from the fire wafting up and circling around until a draft would send it outside, rising above the big door.

Beside the fire pot was a big anvil, on which the blacksmith would form and shape the horseshoe to fit the horse's hoof. At the foot of the anvil was a pail of water for dipping the hot shoe to cool it off.

To the best of my recollection, Julian Perry was rather short in stature but muscular. He was bald and wore a black, peakless cap and sported a handlebar mustache. This man never reprimanded us kids because we usually kept out of his way and just watched.

It was fascinating to watch as the smithy sidled up to the horse, picked up one of the animal's legs, and held it between and above his knees. He would take a large pair of pliers and pull off the old horseshoe and its nails. Then he would file and fit the horse's hoof before forming a new horseshoe. At that point there was the banging and clanking of the hammer on the anvil as the shoe was heated in the fire, then formed for the hoof.

The horse would usually stand still for a few minutes, and if it didn't, the blacksmith or the horse's owner barked a few choice, blunt words, then yanked on the horse's bit to bring it back into line.

After watching a couple of shoeings, we would drift on to another place, another game, and another world—maybe it was "cowboys and Indians," or, if we had enough kids, maybe "2 o'cat or 3 o'cat" (softball).

1942-43

Early in the morning, when I was 13 or 14, one of my chores was to feed five or six chickens we kept in the backyard near the garage. These white leghorn birds would start out as little chicks that Dad brought home from someone he knew at work at the Rochester Button Co. Seems as though it was my job. So I would get the mash and the oyster shell to feed them and water them. Soon they were laying eggs at a rate faster than we ate them. I sort of had an aversion to eating the eggs, and most probably it was because I was attached to the chickens.

Was that possible? I asked myself. Anyway, we had eggs, certainly not enough to sell but more than we could handle. Someone told me about "Water Glass," a powdery material in an envelope that you put into a 5-gallon crock. You mix the solvent and put the eggs into the 5 gallons and cover the top, keeping it in a cool, dark place. These eggs seemed to keep for maybe a couple of months or longer.

Speaking of eggs, Bill Kirk, a farmer and school bus driver who lived outside the village, used to raise chickens that laid eggs with different-colored yolks. He had a secret that no one ever found out. I tried to do it by putting food coloring in the mash, but it didn't work. Bill went on a radio program called *Vox Pop,* in 1939 or 1940, telling about his hobby. In those days, anyone who went on national radio was a real celebrity. Bill was a World War I veteran and one of the early members of the American Legion.

Reminiscing about the radio shows like *Vox Pop,* I can remember others such as *Hobby Lobby, Easy Aces* ("Ladies and gentlemen..."), *Mr. Keene, Tracer of Lost Persons* (its theme song was Noel Coward's "Somewhere I'll Find You..."), *John J. Anthony* (solver of personal problems), *Fibber McGee & Molly, Duffy's Tavern* ("where the elite meet to eat"), *Lux Radio Theater, Inner Sanctum, The Shadow,* Arch Oboler's *Lights Out,* and many others. Listening to those programs, a person could conjure up his or her own vision of the characters and scenes depicted. The advantage of radio was that you could listen to it and still be doing something else, whereas with television, you're a slave to listening and watching.

We had an old Atwater-Kent radio in the living room, and we would listen to it in the late afternoon. There would be children's programs such as *Jack Armstrong, the All-American Boy, Little Orphan Annie, Tom Mix* (a cowboy), and later *Captain Midnight.* I even remember that Wheaties, the "Breakfast of Champions," sponsored *Jack Armstrong,* and the opening and ending song went like this: "We, the Piper Hudson High boys, show them how we stand/We excel in being champions known throughout the la-a-a-a-and."

1943

My father bought an old "highboy" radio for $2 once. We cut it down by cutting about 8 or 10 inches off the legs. That made it a little lighter, too. The thing weighed a "ton" because it had a heavy powerpack with transformers and coils used for the speaker. I was able to tune in only three stations. One was WHAM, a 50,000-watt "clear channel station," which meant that no other station could be on that frequency in the U.S. The other two stations were WHEC and WSAY. Gordon Brown owned and operated this small station for many years, and the radiated power was probably not more than 250-500 watts.

I had the radio in my room, and it gave me much enjoyment when I was a teenager. At the end of World War II, new appliances started to come on the market. I bought a GE table model. It worked well at times and sometimes not, because it had a very sensitive loop antenna. You had to move it around to get the best reception. Whether I realized it or not, I was being exposed to the principles of RDF (Radio Direction Finding), a theory I learned later in the Coast Guard Radio School.

III. HIGH SCHOOL

Class Day 1944 found us freshmen singing, "We're a ramblin' wreck from Hilton High and a heck of a freshman class" to the tune of "Ramblin' Wreck from Georgia Tech."

A sad event occurred in March 1944 when Harvey's best friend, Joe Kelley, was killed in an Air Corps training mission down in Louisiana. Joe had graduated from high school in 1943, enlisted in the Army Air Corps, and trained as a top turret gunner in a B-17. He went up for a ride in a B-24 that crashed on takeoff with full fuel and burned. That traumatic event brought the reality of war home to our family and many Hiltonites who knew the Kelley family.

Harvey was in the Marines at the time, and when he was told about it, he was devastated for some time. Harvey and Joe had been inseparable before the war.

"Topping corn" was a summer job we teenage boys had for maybe six to eight weeks every year. Around 1943-45, when we were 14 to 16 years old, the Grange League Federation, a farmers' cooperative, would hire boys at 25 to 35 cents an hour to work in their cornfields. The GLF was experimenting with hybrid field corn. They would plant four rows of female corn, then one row of male corn throughout an entire field. The female corn was "topped," meaning detasseled from the top of the stalks, until the cornsilk started to show on the ears. Then, much later in the summer, the male rows pollinated the female rows.[*]

This project had been going on for some time, because Harvey "topped corn" in 1941. He worked at the canning factory (Smithfield's Pure Food Co.) that fall, then joined the Marines just before Pearl Harbor.

Bright and early, we guys took our lunches in hand and met in the center of the village, on Main Street, to wait for the GLF field boss to pick us up. Brownie, as we called him, had a good rapport with us, and

---

[*]When I talked with an agricultural research group recently, they asserted that they "try for 98 percent" in their program.

he put up with a lot from us, too. He would pile maybe eight or nine of us in his car, and we would drive out in the country to the cornfields, which were scattered all around the northwestern part of the county in a radius of about 10 miles from Hilton.

Once in the field, we would be assigned to two rows, one on each side. Working our way through, we pulled the tassels off the stalks and discarded them on the ground. When the field was finished, we would pile back into the car and go to another field, maybe a mile or as many as 10 miles away. Usually there was an older boy who had an old car or jalopy, and some of us would ride with him.

That kept us busy seven or eight hours a day, five days a week, because after a field was topped, the tassels grew back after a few days. We had to go over the same fields several times. We'd earn, maybe, $15 to $20 a week, which was good money for teenagers at that time.

Of course, when a bunch of boys get together, there's always a lot of horseplay. We were no different, and there was a lot of fooling around in the fields. Some of the guys thought they were grown up, and they were able to get cigarettes, even in wartime. Smoking was common with many, and sometimes, while they were fooling around, a lighted cigarette would be dropped into another fellow's back pocket, and he could get burned.

Once we heard a blood-curdling scream, and when we raced over to this friend of mine, we found his pants and handkerchief in flames. He got quite a burn and scar from that "prank." Brownie put a stop to that kind of shenanigans, at least for a while.

At times, fights broke out among us kids, mostly caused by friction between some city (Rochester) kids and us villagers. As it turned out, city kids did not work out too well because they always found ways to get out of working. They were connivers, always tricky, cunning, and devious. Brownie sent them back after a week and told them they were all through.

I used to help out on a farm that is now a housing development on the east side of Hilton. John Curtis, an elderly retired farmer, lived with his daughter and her family across the street from where I lived. "Grandpa" Curtis owned that farm, and John Heise and his family lived on the farm and operated it. Zeke Kelley and I liked to work there because Mr. Heise would let us drive the team of horses occasionally. I worked there after school or on Saturdays, hoeing beans; picking sour cherries, apples, and tomatoes; and pruning trees in the orchards in the early spring. More than once, Zeke and I pitched hay off the wagon into the barn.

Our high school principal, Cecil Luffman, who had lost his right arm at the elbow years earlier, would help out part-time on the farm, too. Even with his handicap, he could work alongside any able-bodied man, play basketball, or do anything else.

On one particular hot, humid, stifling summer day, Mr. Luffman had brought a few bottles of beer from the local beer joint, the Arlington Hotel in the village. He offered Mr. Heise a beer as we all stood around and took a mid-afternoon break, and I guess Zeke and I looked like a couple of disheveled beggars with our tongues hanging out. It was very hot, and we were sweaty and dirty and covered with hay chaff, which makes your skin itch all over.

"Walters, can you and Kelley handle a beer?" Mr. Luffman asked with a half-hearted laugh.

Old John Heise laughed, too, as he spat tobacco juice through his three-day growth of gray beard. It dripped down the bib of his overalls.

"Yes, sir," I replied. "We can handle anything if it's cold and wet!"

Zeke and I shared a bottle of beer, my first taste of it at age 14. The school principal had offered us our first beer—and I liked it! But I never touched another one until I was 21.

Occasionally I spaded gardens for neighbors in the spring, and I usually had three lawns to mow every week. One day in early April 1945, I was spading a garden for Mr. Mikel, a neighbor, after school. When my father got home from work, he came over to the Mikels' yard and gave me the day's big news: "President Roosevelt died suddenly this afternoon." Everyone seemed to be in a state of incredulous disbelief or profound shock, just as they were years later when President Kennedy was shot.

During the war years 1943-45, I delivered the *Rochester Democrat & Chronicle,* a morning newspaper. Getting up early was never a problem for me. I could wake up at 6 or 6:30 a.m. and peddle the 40 or 50 dailies on the east side of the village. Around 7 a.m. I would return home to have breakfast with my mother and leave for school at about 7:30 a.m. Walking through the village to school took about 12 minutes, and classes started at about 8 a.m.

I prided myself on folding the newspapers so they were about 3 by 12 inches. Then I would throw them from the front sidewalk up onto the customer's front porch, which was maybe 25 to 30 feet distant. Once, I remember, my throw went high and up on the customer's roof. Needless to say, my folks did not get their paper that day because I had to give theirs to the customer.

My travels during the early morning took me past the stores on Main Street. Gradually I got to know everyone doing their early morning duties: Red, the milkman, delivering for Smith's Dairy; Hans, the Wonder Bread deliveryman; and Fred, who ran the Flying Red A gas station, plus others that I remember well. Sometimes on a cold winter morning, Red would stop his truck and give me a ride down the street to my next customer. That would get me out of the weather for a couple of minutes.

One clear morning, as I was walking along, a car pulled over to the curb and a voice called out, "Young man, come here!"

I walked over to the car, where two men were in the front and two ladies were in the back. I had never seen them before, and in a small village of 900 people, you knew everyone in those days.

The driver asked me, "Can you tell me what that tower is over there?"

He pointed to the south and the two towers on South Hill. One was the old village water tower, and the other was a 200-foot tower erected by the Bausch & Lomb Co., which to my knowledge had been built by them for testing lenses in Rochester about 12 miles away. The driver spoke with a definite foreign accent, and the others were speaking in the same accent among themselves. I detected something odd, so I said I didn't know what the tower was.

As they drove on slowly, I began to wonder why they were so curious. When I finished my paper route, I went to a next-door neighbor who was a sheriff's detective and told him everything that happened, giving him their license plate number, which I had memorized.

I never heard that anything came of this incident. The strangers' questions were probably innocent, but I felt I had done my patriotic duty, which made me feel pretty good. If something had happened and I had said nothing, I would have felt like a traitor.

The hardest part of the newspaper delivery was collecting money from the customers each week. I always collected at the same time— Friday evenings and Saturday mornings. Most of the customers were very good about paying their bills, which amounted to maybe 45 to 70 cents, depending on whether they took the Sunday paper. But there was one lady who never seemed to have enough change. She'd always say to me, "You probably don't have change, do you?" Then she would flash a $10 bill at me. That meant I had to scrape up enough change every week and make a special trip, going back to her a second time to collect.

One week I was ready for her. This time, when she flashed her $10 bill, I said, "Yes, I can make change." As I unloaded my pockets, I counted out 45 pennies, 31 dimes, 20 nickels, 16 quarters, and a $1 bill. She got the message. After that, there was never a problem collecting from her.

Every year at Christmas time, the newspaper company put out calendars for us newsboys to buy for about 25 cents each. The idea was to pass out these calendars to our customers as Christmas gifts, and the customers would reciprocate in kind and give us gifts. Some were very generous and would give us maybe a couple of dollars or a billfold; those who couldn't afford much would give only $1. What you got depended on the service you gave the customers throughout the year. I'm sure no one ever gave me less than 50 cents.

Except a drugstore owner who owned a block of stores and a few private homes. Approaching him in his store one day, I asked if he would like the annual D&C calendar. He replied, "Well, yes, certainly," as he took it out of my hand and walked to the back room. He never even thanked me. That hurt, and besides that, I was out 25 cents.

That man sold calendars every year in his drugstore, so it wasn't that he needed one himself. Orange A. Green (believe it or not, that was his real name) was *cheap!*

When I was about 12 or 13, my friend Zeke and I each made a pair of stilts. Mine had steps about 2 feet above the ground. We would walk on those stilts all over the east side of the village.

One day when I was feeling a little bold, I got the bright idea of walking across one of the shallow parts of Salmon Creek. It didn't look like such a bad idea, and it didn't look impossible either. The water ran fast because it was shallow and the creek had a stony bottom.

Approaching the bank warily, I very carefully stepped down into the water. I took two short steps, and everything was fine. But two steps later, into the rushing water while trying to get a footing on some slippery stones—well, that proved to me that it was not such a good idea.

Sssppp—lash! Down I went, sprawled halfway across the creek. I should have known enough to fall toward the bank and not into the middle of the creek.

I was soaked and my stilts went floating down the creek. I pursued them and then had to trudge all the way home—soaking wet!

When I delivered the morning papers, one of my customers on East Avenue was B. A. Haines, who by some villagers' standards was "a bit eccentric." He fancied himself an artist, and as a 15-year-old, who was I to critique his work? Older folks had their own ideas, I'm sure.

Mr. Haines had also built a cottage at Lighthouse Beach, near Hilton. One hot summer day, my friend Zeke Kelley and his family, who were neighbors of the Haineses, asked me to go with them to visit the Haineses for a day at the beach.

This cottage was a revolutionary design in its day, probably equal to one of Frank Lloyd Wright's homes. In the center of the main floor, there was a fireplace open on both sides, one side in the kitchen and the other in the living room. The second-floor bedrooms were laid out around the edge of the circular house, which was open in the middle—what today we call a "cathedral ceiling." It was quite unique at that time, I thought.

Mr. Haines was probably in his mid-to-late 80s; he was about the same age as my grandfather. One Saturday afternoon when I was collecting on my paper route, I rang the Haineses' doorbell, and Mrs. Haines, a kindly old lady, asked me to step in so she could shut the door.

As we stood in the vestibule so she could count out the change, Mr. Haines came up and asked me, "Say, young man, have I ever told you about the time I trained horses for Custer's army?"

Before I could answer, Mrs. Haines interrupted. "This boy doesn't want to hear about you years ago, and he certainly doesn't have time to listen to your stories."

I replied, "No, I would like to hear about it."

Embarrassed, Mrs. Haines remained quiet as her husband began his story.

"As a boy, I was born and raised in the Midwest," he said. "I grew up and helped my father train horses. The cavalry came by and took some of those we trained, and they were used in the U.S. Army for Custer's campaigns. Just think! Some of those horses were probably used at the Battle of Little Big Horn!"

I remarked that I thought that was very interesting. Mr. Haines seemed to revel in telling me his little story. Other customers sometimes had to tell me a story before I could get out of their houses, but they weren't all that interesting.

Mr. Haines absolutely detested dogs because he had cats and didn't like any dogs in his yard. If any dog wandered into his yard, he would throw sharpened spears at them.

My dog Lucky, a springer spaniel, and I were playing at Zeke Kelley's one day, and Lucky went into the Haineses' yard. Old man Haines came stumbling out of the house and off his back porch, throwing his spears at Lucky. The dog just circled around Haines, staying out of reach of his spears. I had all I could do to call Lucky out of Haines's yard and get him back into the Kelleys' yard.

Haines hated dogs so much, he would collect dog feces that appeared along the front of his property and pile it on his sidewalk, then leave a note in chalk for people to see.

One hot, humid summer day at Zeke's, Mr. Kelley called us boys and said, "Look at that!" Seems that another neighbor's dog, Pal, was sitting smack dab in the middle of a wash pan half full of water in Haines's yard, near his back porch. Pal was from an older litter of the same bitch that bore Lucky. Pal was not known to be very smart; he was never trained and never came when called, but he did know enough to cool off on a hot day. There he sat in that basin just keeping cool. Haines never saw him, and Pal must have sat there for 10 minutes. Then he climbed out, shook himself off, and left the yard.

1945: I was about 16 years old when this picture was taken.

My high school years were quite happy for the most part. My closest friends were Zeke Kelley and Art Verney. Art was in the same class with me. Jim Daily and I often chummed around together after 1939. He came from a broken home, quit high school, and joined the Navy at the war's end. When he was discharged, he lived with my parents and me for a couple of years until I went in the service.

SPORTS

I never went out much for sports in high school. I always figured I wasn't good enough. When you are never encouraged by your folks, it becomes a fact of life. We guys played sandlot ball all the time, but in a small town you never could find more than four or five guys at the most to play. So we had to play one-o-cat or two-o-cat mostly. I should have

May 1947: Three cool dudes, left to right— "Tony" Walters, Zeke Kelley, and Chuck Beaty.

gone out for the team anyway, because I could see that I was probably as good as the others who played.

One spring day in my senior year, 1947, the school team was to journey down the road to Spencerport for a ball game. Len Wright, the high school coach, our home room adviser, history and law teacher, and my longtime neighbor, called me aside between classes that afternoon. He said to go get a uniform and be ready to get on the team bus with them. I remember all the guys yelling for me, and they were glad to see me joining the team. I felt pretty good, and right then I knew what I had lost all those years.

That game remains quite vivid to me even after 50 years. Playing right field, I misjudged the first fly ball hit into my area as my good friend Art backed me up. After that I caught a couple of flies and returned a couple singles to second base. Art was noticing I was not throwing the ball very well; he mentioned it to me on the bench after the first inning. I showed him the splint on the middle finger of my right (throwing) hand. That noon hour, at school, I had jumped up to catch a fly ball and caught the end of my finger. The last joint of my finger was bent down at a 90-degree angle. I was sent to my doctor, and he put a splint on it; it was what he called a "good sprain."

I enjoyed talking to Grandpa Skinner, even though he was quite deaf. He would yell at me to repeat what I said and to speak louder. Many kids talk too fast, mumble their words, and do not look often enough at the listener.

There were no hits by our team until I came up in the third (undoubtedly batting ninth). I got a hit to center to start things off. Later I was hit by the pitcher and drew a walk, which meant I batted 1,000 for the game and the year. That was my claim to glory. Len gave me a baseball letter for the year.

Grandpa would tell me about when he was a boy growing up. He had lived on farmland, which is now part of Rochester, New York, near the Genesee River. Eastman Kodak now owns the property, which borders Ridge Road and Lake Avenue. In Grandpa's day it was called Hanford Landing. He told me that when he was a little kid, maybe 10 or

12 years old, he would go out and stand on big boulders and jump down on top of snakes to kill them with his high leather boots.

When he was about 4 (I figure that was about 1863), the Civil War was in full swing. Grandpa's oldest brother, William, was in the Union Army fighting at that time. Grandpa's father took him down to the New York Central Railroad station where President Abraham Lincoln was evidently campaigning for his second term. Papa Skinner held young DeWitt up on his shoulders so the young lad could see the President at the rear of the train.

I remember that as clearly as the day Grandpa told me the story, when I was 14 or 15. Passing it on to my mother and other relatives, years after Grandpa had died, I found that no one else recalled hearing the story. I suspect that many children and grandchildren do not care to hear what an old man relates along with a little nostalgia.

My cousin Howard and I were Grandpa Skinner's two youngest grand-children. With no male descendants to carry on the Skinner name, the DeWitt Clinton Skinner lineage stops with Cousin Gordon.

Grandpa Skinner died in April 1949 while I was serving in the U.S. Coast Guard on a ship in the Pacific.

1944 POWS

Trekking down Main Street about 7 a.m. on my paper route, I heard a roar behind me, getting louder and louder. Glancing over my shoulder, I could see the two-ton truck speeding down West Avenue from the west. It was used to transport German prisoners of war from the POW Camp in the old Civilian Conservation Corps Camp in Hamlin. After the war, that camp was turned into what is now Hamlin Beach State Park.

That day the truck came careening through the village; the guards must have been late. As I watched, the truck swerved rather sharply to make its turn from Main Street to East Avenue, which was on a left oblique angle, and I distinctly remember that the left side and wheels rose off the ground by six inches or more. Those POWs must have experienced quite a ride that day; they were darned lucky.

Every fall, Smithfield's Pure Foods Co., better known as the "canning factory," processed applesauce. The POW truck was headed for the factory, where the German POWs were put to work outside shoveling apples under Army guards. They would shovel the apples into troughs, like viaducts, which carried the apples into the plant for processing. We teenagers who lived on the east side would go down to the factory and watch the prisoners; sometimes the guards would shoo us away.

Those Germans were Hitler's "super race," his blond, blue-eyed "cream of the crop," who had surrendered or been captured in North Africa. POWs were paid 80 cents a day, according to the Geneva Convention (international law). The way those Germans played around, I don't think they were worth any more than that. They wore dungaree shirts and pants that had large white "PW" letters on them. Not many tried to escape throughout the whole United States, and some did not want to go back home after the war was over.

Two or three years later, I was working on the apple pile after school when I was 16 or 17. I shoveled apples for only a short time before I was called to work in the warehouse. That was what every young man aspired to in those days, if he wanted to work in Hilton. We packed cans in cases (we called it "picking"), glued flaps, and stenciled and stacked cases in piles and more piles. In the meantime we enjoyed it and were getting paid 65 cents an hour.

As teenagers, we worked maybe from 4 to 10 p.m. on weekdays and from 8 a.m. to 5 or 6 p.m. on Saturdays. We might earn $15 or $25 a week, depending on the amount of work available.

My mother expected $10 a week from me for room and board. If I made $12, she still expected and got the $10. Other classmates I knew did not have to give any money to their parents. When Jim Daily lived with us, he worked full-time at the canning factory. He worked 60 or 70 hours a week, making $35 to $40. Mother asked Jim for $10 a week, the same as she got from me. I didn't complain; I thought it was my fair share, because I knew others who had it much worse than me. I always managed to buy small things I needed and eventually my own clothes. When I graduated from high school in 1947, I got a job at Eastman Kodak starting at $40 a week, and Mother told me I could afford to pay her $15, then $20. Jim still paid only $15. Mother said I could afford it better than he could.

Oh, well.

ICE SKATING

As a teenager in the winter, I used to go ice skating quite frequently. On Firemen's Field on South Avenue in Hilton, the area between the creek and the current firehouse, the land was not filled in those days. It was low land, and the firemen would flood an area of maybe 80 feet square for skating. It provided much entertainment for skaters in the winter. On crisp, cold nights we had a ball.

Occasionally, one of my classmates, Bob Woodams, would get his father's Model A Ford and drive into the village to pick me up. We would round up a few other guys, pick up our skates, and take off to a secluded pond for an evening of fun.

Often somebody would say, "Let's skate up North Creek and take Walker by surprise." Walker was a hamlet of about 20 houses and a general store. Bob would have the manifold heater blasting out the heat as we tooled across the icy, snow-slicked roads for four miles to Walker. It was our halfway point when we drove up to the front of Pete Foos's General Store. Inside we would always find Pete, Mrs. Foos, and their two sons, Carl and Billy, sitting around a table playing euchre.

We would banter a bit with the Fooses, buy a nickel candy bar (my favorite was a Clark Bar) and a nickel Coke, then take off for our evening adventure.

About four miles farther was a farmer's pond located near Lake Ontario. The owner had apple orchards for the most part, and the area was where they developed and grew the world's largest apple, the 20-ounce apple, which made the most delicious apple pies and applesauce.

This pond had a few cattails, but it was the largest skating rink I had ever seen. We usually built a fire and drank our Cokes. What more could anyone ask for? No one was around to bother us, and we were out of the way of adults. In those days, kids were to be "seen but not heard," and sometimes adults wanted them out of the way, too.

On another occasion, when we were seniors, Bob and I and a couple of others decided to drive to another village to check out the girls. It was quite late, maybe 10 or 11 p.m. How many girls were going to be out at that hour, especially in the winter?

It was a bright, clear moonlit night and so cold the snow crunched under the tires as we drove along. We decided to drive to Churchville, which had to be 12 miles away, and we also decided to drive the entire round trip by moonlight—no car lights. We didn't see any girls at that time of night, but as we left the village, we passed a farmhouse where a girl we knew lived. So we tooted the horn, and she opened her upstairs bedroom window so we could talk for a few minutes until she got cold. Luckily her father didn't come out to chase us off.

All was not lost, so we drove back to Hilton. It was exhilarating, tooling around in an old Model A, late at night. Can you imagine driving nowadays at 11 o'clock at night on a paved road for even one mile with no lights? There simply was not much traffic then compared to the way it is now, and we knew all the side roads.

CARAMEL SUCKERS

A caramel sucker was my favorite candy when I was a little boy. A caramel sucker cost one penny. A caramel sucker would last me for an hour. When my grandfather came to visit, he would always give each of us kids a penny. When he left, I would run to the candy store for—a caramel sucker.

The Pleasure Shop was the local candy store where we would buy our penny candy. "Louie's," or the Hilton Candy Kitchen on Main Street, was an excellent place for homemade chocolates or homemade ice cream.

Louie and Mrs. Panarites emigrated to the United States after World War I and settled in Hilton. They had six children, three girls and three boys; all the boys served in the Army in World War II. Manuel, the youngest, was in school at the same time I was, and Nick, the middle boy, eventually took over the family business until retiring in the 1980s.

There was a little-known but very true story about Louie Panarites that occurred during the Depression in the early 1930s. It seems that Louie was standing outside his storefront one evening when a local Hiltonite happened by. The two exchanged greetings, then Louie remarked, "You come on in my place and have some ice cream."

The fellow replied, "Louie, I can't. I don't have any money."

Louie responded, "Yes, yes, come on in and have some ice cream anyways. If I can't sell it, I might as well give it away."

I have no doubt about the authenticity of that story because I know that Louie gave ice cream to many of us when we were kids.

As we grew up, my friends and I frequented Louie's during the years we were in high school. My good friend Art Verney and I walked from the high school (located on the West side) through the village on the way home every day. Quite often another classmate, Smitty, would join us as we stopped at Louie's for ice cream. Grabbing a booth in the back, we would order our favorite dishes. Art would ask for a lemon frappé, Smitty would get maybe a Blackeyed Susan, and I always ordered a Mexican.

Art and I would sit in the booth facing the front windows, looking out onto Main Street. Smitty, never realizing our motives, always sat on the other side facing the back of the store.

Either Art or I would say, "Hey, Smitty, get a load of Pat (or Nancy or Shirley) across the street. She looks sharp!"

Invariably Smitty would turn, look around, and always leave his ice cream unguarded. Art and I usually ate half his dish every time. To this day, I don't believe he was ever the wiser.

FALL 1946

The Class of 1947 put on plays when we were sophomores, juniors, and seniors. We all had a ball doing it under the direction of our assistant homeroom teacher, Miss Olive Durant. She taught the businesscourses at the high school. She also assisted our homeroom teacher, Leonard Wright, who taught history and law and coached varsity baseball.

In the early fall, those of us interested in dramatics tried out for parts in the short plays. As sophomores and juniors, our plays were only one act, each lasting about 45 minutes. The Senior Play, *June Mad,* was a comedy in three acts, lasting about an hour and a half, not counting intermissions.

The most exciting part of it all was auditioning for the roles and re-hearsing after school, week after week. We probably rehearsed at least three afternoons a week after school, from 3 to 5 p.m.

If we were not in the scene that was being rehearsed, we boys would g out the back door of the stage, which was actually our gymnasium, sit on the steps, and get a breath of fresh air. When a scene was finished and Miss Durant, sitting in the middle of the auditorium, would call out for another scene to be rehearsed, she would have someone call us back inside for our scenes.

One nice, warm fall afternoon, we were out on the back steps fooling around and kidding, as boys always do. I spotted an old half-pint whis-key bottle on the ground near the steps. Someone picked it up, and we were looking at it, when suddenly the door burst open as one of the girls called us inside. We were a little startled, and as we walked in, someone handed me the bottle and I simply stuck it in my right rear pocket.

The scene began as I entered stage left, and I started talking about how great I was, comparing myself to an old-time movie actor, Wally Reid. Actually I had only a minor part, about 90 lines. I was playing the father of the main character, played by my friend Ken Slater.

I turned to face the mirror on the wall as I was talking about myself, and I completely forgot *everything* in the script. As I rambled on and ad-libbed about how good I thought I was—it seemed like minutes—I heard a voice in the background, seemingly miles away.

"Elmer—Elmer—*Elmer! What are you doing?"*

I stopped suddenly, turned toward that darkened auditorium, and saw a pair of eyes blazing away, piercing right through me!

"What in heaven's name are you *doing?* I don't read that in *my* script!"

"Oh, I'm sorry, Miss Durant," I said, noticing that the other actors had entered the stage, laughing at me.

At that point, Miss Durant happened to notice something that was not a prop.

"Elmer—what have you got in your rear pants pocket?"

I stopped for a moment. *What is she talking about?* I wondered, and then it struck me. *Oh, my gosh! That bottle is still in my pocket!*

"Elmer, get rid of that—whatever it is!"

I apologized to Miss Durant and discarded the bottle in a trash can outside. My school friends laughed and kidded me about that. Miss Durant never mentioned that episode to me again either.

Actually performing the plays was not as exciting as the camaraderie of auditioning and rehearsing, much as planning a trip is often more fun than the trip itself.

Of course the last night was fun because someone always threw a party after the final performance of the play. We all had dates, and we sat around and rehashed the performance and laughed at all our goofs. Miss Durant was still trying to find out who put a derby hat on top of the maid's laundry cart in the third act on our last night (in front of parents and friends).

I'm still not about to tell, but it did draw a few laughs.

In late May 1947, a bunch of us senior boys hopped into Bob Woodams' Model A Ford and drove up to Spencerport, our football rival. After it was dark, we were going to check out the local girls, but they were nowhere to be seen, so we happened to turn up at Spencerport High School. Out back we saw some temporary 2-by-4 goalposts, which we thought marked the boys' soccer or touch football field. As a joke on the Spencerport High boys, we worked the posts loose and tore them down, then left immediately, hoping that no one had seen us.

A few days later, Bob, Zeke, Peewee, and I were cruising in the late afternoon after school in downtown Spencerport. We had just passed the old firehouse on Main Street when we spied a couple of Spencerport senior girls, so we pulled over to the curb.

Graduation: Hilton High School's Class of 1947. I'm fourth from the right in the third row.

We were all making small talk when one of the girls asked if we had heard the news. "Our principal has barred all the senior boys from intramural sports for the rest of the year. He accused them of tearing down the goalposts in back of the school. Those boys were terrible!"

"No kidding!" Bob and I pretended to be surprised, but we had a hard time not laughing. Zeke and Peewee were lowerclassmen, so they weren't in on the prank. They were really surprised at the news until later when Bob and I told them our secret.

GRADUATION

Graduation from high school in June 1947 was a happy event, and yet it was sad. We were all happy because we wondered what lay ahead, and yet we were sad because we were "breaking up that old gang." I interviewed for a job at a large bank in Rochester and was hired. I could see myself in banking for 40 or more years. Then Kodak offered more money, almost double the amount, so I went to Kodak. I worked in the Cine Processing Lab, which developed 8- and 16-mm amateur film.

I checked all the recruiting offices through the summer, and they all wanted to sign me up right away, except the Coast Guard. They wouldn't talk to me because they weren't taking anyone—they had a full quota.

Later in August 1947, Kodak offered me a new assignment. They wanted me to train as a "densitometer technician" in the same lab, creating a new position. They took me to the Research Lab and introduced me to the inventor of the densitometer, a machine that measured light density of colored film strips. It measured the density of the three basic colors in film: yellow, magenta, and cyan.

Color film strips were run through the developing baths of each machine every hour. I would collect the strips from each machine hourly, test them on the densitometer, then mark a chart on each machine. These charts would then indicate the strength or weakness of the solutions. Other lab techs in our department would either add to or dilute the chemicals to control the correct colors of the film.

This promised a good future for the right person, but after four months I told Kodak that I felt I had an obligation to my government and to myself to get out and see the world. At 18, I honestly could not see working shift work for 40 or more years in the same brick building.

I just had to see what was "on the other side of the hill." Some of my friends and relatives asked, "Why do you want to quit Kodak with a good job and promising future to join the military?" There was no draft; the government had stopped it in February 1947. That may have been very well, but I had two brothers who had fought in World War II, and I felt it was my obligation to serve, too.

After leaving Eastman Kodak in November 1947, I received my orders to report to the 9th Coast Guard District Office on Euclid Avenue in Cleveland, Ohio. I said my good-byes, kissed my mother, and bade farewell to my dog, Lucky. My brother-in-law, Pete, who was working the afternoon shift at Kodak, took me into Rochester, where I boarded the New York Central for Cleveland.

I must confess that I was a bit apprehensive and don't remember much of the trip, except learning how to use government meal tickets aboard trains. The next day I was sworn in by a Coast Guard commander. Afterward, he said he was going to give me my first order.

"Seaman Walters, go to the theater and see a good movie and enjoy yourself. Your train leaves at 6 p.m. for Florida."

There was a layover in Washington, DC the next day, so, with a couple of hours to spare, I walked around. I saw quite a few Marines in the city, and for a fleeting moment I sort of wished I had joined the Marines as my big brother had. It struck me all of a sudden because I had signed up for four years in the Coast Guard, and all the other services had only three-year hitches.

Coming back to my senses, I told myself, "What am I thinking? I joined because the Coast Guard has the most meaningful purpose, in my mind: saving life and property at sea."

It was, after all, peacetime. I figured the chances of getting the type of work I wanted and making promotions were the best. To this day I have never regretted it.

Don't get me wrong—up until the day I first visited the Coast Guard Recruiting Office in Rochester, I had wanted to be a soldier in the tank corps. My older brother Bob was drafted into the Army before Pearl Harbor. He said, "Never join the Army, because you walk all the time and live in foxholes."

My younger brother Harvey, who joined the Marines at Pearl Harbor, said, "The Navy is what you should join. In the Navy you have a warm bunk, hot food, and you can learn a trade." I think he was a Navy man at heart.

But I said, "I'm no swimmer!"

Harvey said, "Hell, they'll teach you. You just grab your privates with the left hand and hold your nose with the right hand and jump 20 feet into the pool."

I didn't want to go to sea, or so I thought, but after my first sea duty in 1948, all I wanted was a ship under me.

My two hours of walking around and day-dreaming were over, so I boarded an Atlantic Coast Line train bound for Jacksonville, Fla.

BOOT CAMP

When I arrived in Jacksonville, a Coast Guard jeep picked up another recruit and me. The other recruit, an Army veteran, was from North Carolina, and I was to find out soon that 80 percent of the Coast Guard is composed of North Carolinians—at least it certainly seemed that way.

We were driven to the Mayport CG boot camp, which was formerly the Navy Air Station on the St. Johns River. The Coast Guard had the base there for a short time, and then the Navy took it back in 1948.

We were mess cooks for the first two weeks until enough recruits were accumulated to form a platoon of 30. Not many fellows were enlisting just before the holiday season. We were known as "Company R," and soon after New Year's Day 1948, we formed two platoons of 30 men each; the 1st and 2nd platoons were then ready for training.

Chief Finnan, and old-time signalman, was our company commander, and GM1 Fitch was his assistant. Both men were good teachers and kept us pretty much in line. We had to know the 10 General Orders the first day before we could go to the post movie. "To walk my post in a military manner, keeping always on the alert and observing everything within sight or hearing" was the first order. Don't ask me what the others were.

SPECIAL ASSIGNMENT

Two weeks after classes of knot tying, seamanship, rowing the 26-foot monomoy lifeboats, Coast Guard history, some maritime rules and regulations, and marching up and down the airstrip plus manual-of-arms, the instructor called me aside one day. He had a special request for someone who had experience in typing and had an aptitude for interviewing people. I seemed to be the only eligible candidate, according to the enlistment forms. I was assigned to work in the recruits' office, where a petty officer and I interviewed new recruits and filled out their basic forms (*i.e.,* name, address, blood type, dependents, next of kin, *etc.*).

While my Company R buddies were marching up and down the strip with their M1s out in the cold rain, I had to sit at my desk in the office and listen to Arthur Godfrey or Paul Whiteman's orchestra all day long.

I must have done a fairly good job because when the time came for Company R to graduate, the base wanted me to consider staying there and striking for a rating.

I said, "No, if it's all the same, I would just as soon go to school." No schooling was available at that time, so I requested General Sea Duty.

As the last two members of the 1st Platoon, Matashowski (known as "Ski"), from Pittsburgh, and I were shipped out to a ship in Seattle, Wash., assigned to the *CGC Unalga,* later to be known as the "Mighty U" or the "Dirty U" and at times as the "Black Witch" (at one time the ship had been painted black).

V. THE 'MIGHTY U'

Ski and I were sent on Pullmans by the Atlantic Seaboard and Milwaukee Railroads from Jacksonville to Seattle. The trip took about four days, and we then had to take a bus ride of about 30 miles to Everett, Wash., where our ship was tied up.

My first impression of the ship was "Ugh! What a dirty scow!" She was being repainted, and within the next month, the "Dirty U" looked more like the "Mighty U."

CGC UNALGA

The Coast Guard Cutter *Unalga* was classed as an AK cargo ship of 365 feet in length. The beam was probably 65 to 70 feet wide. She had two large hatches forward with cargo booms and a smaller hatch behind the superstructure with smaller cargo booms. The *Unalga* and her sister ship, the *Kukui,* were the largest ships in the Coast Guard. A buddy of mine in boot camp, Earl ("Tex") Schulte of Goose Creek, Texas (now NASA Space Center), was assigned to the *Kukui,* which serviced the 14th CGD.

On the *Unalga,* I met and made a good friend from Rochester, N.Y., Al Lentzer. Al went to Edison Tech High School, where he knew my Uncle Walt, who taught photography there. Al was involved in the "deck force group" that later went over the hill for 29 days in August 1948. He had gone in the service before me, but he ended up making his AWOL time up after his enlistment. We later got together in 1952 when we were both out of the service, but I lost track of him.

On one of the first days I was aboard, the deck division was standing in formation for muster, along with about 20 other seamen and three or four bos'n's mates. Chief Petty Officer Harkins took the reports, then reported to the Warrant Bosun, who was in charge of our division. The Chief Warrant Bosun's name was Beverly Higgins—yes, I said "Beverly"—a fairly obvious sign that his mother had wanted a girl. He was a rough and tough old grizzled type of fellow, probably because he had had to fight all his life with a name like that. Years later, country singer Johnny Cash recorded a song, "A Boy Named Sue," which always reminded me of Beverly, the Warrant Bosun.

So there we were at 0800, Muster, Reports, and Colors, and the Warrant Bosun yelled to me, "Hey, you! Where's your foul weather jacket?"

Everyone else had their jackets on, but I had left mine in the berthing quarters. "Sir, mine is downstairs," I answered.

"What did you say?"

"Sir, I left mine downstairs, *Sir!*"

"You left it *where?*"

It finally dawned on me that I had said the wrong thing. Never, *never* use the wrong nomenclature or words in a naval situation. It's not *downstairs,* it's *down below. Walls* and *floors* are *bulkheads* and *decks,* respectively. *Overhead* means *ceiling.*

My buddies in ranks started snickering and laughing at me, and Mr. Higgins shaped them up fast. "Knock it off and wipe those grins off your faces!" Then he turned to me again. "You! What's your name?"

"Walters, *Sir!*"

"Walters, you may *lay below* for your jacket, and I don't mean you can *walk downstairs!*"

For years afterward, even today, I occasionally refer to the *deck,* not the *floor,* and sometimes the *overhead,* not the *ceiling.* I haven't mopped a floor since I was 18, but I have swabbed many decks.

One night a little later I was about to be relieved by another seaman in the crow's nest. He said they were going to secure the crow's nest watch and stand the watch down on the foc'sle (the bow of the ship) because it was too stormy and dangerous to be up in the crow's nest.

I was instructed to take the long overcoat-style parka back to the Bridge. The parka stayed up in the crow's nest at all times. I couldn't figure out how to carry that heavy parka down the mast, with the wind blowing a gale and the heavy snowing, so I thought I'd take off my foul weather jacket and put the heavy parka back on, then throw my jacket down to the main deck, hopefully onto the No. 2 hold deck cover, which was just aft of the mainmast.

1948: The *CGC Unalga,* the 'Mighty U' in all her glory.

To do all that, I had to be standing alongside the crow's nest cubicle. Clinging precariously, I took off my jacket and finally managed to get the parka on. During all the snowing and blowing, the noise of which was deafening, the ship was pitching up and down in 15- to 20-foot waves, and it was rolling up to 35 degrees from port to starboard.

I wadded up my jacket and gave it a heave toward the deck. The jacket left my hand, and immediately the wind caught it and took it out of sight, never to be seen again.

I was seasick at the time and truthfully couldn't have cared less about that jacket. All I cared about was taking that damned parka back to the Bridge and "laying below" to "hit my sack."

In the middle of March 1948, we sailed for Ketchikan, Alaska. It seems that all we did on the deck force was "chip and paint," and then "chip and paint" over it, again and again. During mid-morning or mid-afternoon, we would get a coffee break of 10 minutes. I didn't drink coffee, but I would sit and have a break with my buddies anyway. One of the bos'n's mates would yell at me to get back to work if I wasn't drinking coffee or smoking, like all the other macho men always did. I soon learned to pour a cup of coffee and let it sit there during the break. Eventually I learned to drink the stuff.

Besides working all day, we each had two 4-hour watches to stand, usually 2 hours on the wheel and 2 hours in the crow's nest as lookout. The crow's nest was about 40 feet up the mast located between the two main holds. In all kinds of weather, day or night, we had to climb up the mast and swing over onto the yardarm so the previous watch-stander could climb out and then go back down the mast. Then the new watch-stander would swing over and into the little shelter, where he would stand for the next 2 hours.

One evening, when it was calm, I was standing the wheel watch on the bridge, and I was half listening to the OOD and the quartermaster talking about their wartime experiences at sea. The bos'n's mate told me to relieve the lookout. I left the bridge and went up to the crow's nest for my 2-hour stint.

A short time later, as I was scanning the horizon off the port quarter, I saw what appeared to be a ship on the horizon in the far distance. Then, looking back again, I could see what appeared to be an explosion around that image. It looked just like a ship that had hit a mine that exploded and was burning. I immediately called the bridge on the telephone and reported it to the OOD. As soon as I hung up, I saw the moon rising over the horizon. Was I embarrassed! I tried to avoid that OOD for months afterward. I felt better after learning that such illusions involving the moon are common at sea.

Ketchikan was a small fishing and mining town on the Inside Passage. Its other industry was Creek Street, the "red light" district. Two or three buddies and I walked through the area, but we maintained our innocence, believe it or not. Maybe we didn't have enough money—I don't remember—or maybe we were all too embarrassed to be the first one to step up and talk to the first woman who happened to be standing in a doorway.*

After a few days we sailed across the Gulf of Alaska to Adak Island, midway in the Aleutian chain. Our dockage was in the center part of the harbor, where the Navy was located on the left, the Army base was on the right, and right in the middle were the Marines.

The Marines tried to keep law and order among the three naval services—the Navy, the Coast Guard, and the Marines. Sometimes they had their hands full because some of our Coasties were a pretty rowdy crew. In one incident I remember, about 10 or 15 of the *Unalga* crew went into the Navy beer hall, and after a few beers they stood up on the tables and challenged the whole Navy. The Marines were called in and broke up the fight. No Navy men were detained, but all the Coasties were marched off to the brig. They were prodded with nightsticks all the way, and a few were beaten around the head. They were locked up overnight and released the next day at noon, in the custody of the CO.

No doubt the crew of the *Unalga* was pretty rough. At times when things were dull and peaceful, the crew would fight among themselves. Some had beer or whiskey stashed aboard, and certainly no officer would come in the crew's quarters alone to check it out. Officers never came out on deck or in the crew's quarters at night.

During the noon meal one day, the guys got to throwing food at one another, and it evolved into throwing their trays of food at the plywood movie screen and making quite a mess. The Master-at-Arms stood by and watched the whole affair, doing nothing.

Around that time, a few days before or after, I happened to be the last one through the line at the noon meal. I got my tray of chow and proceeded over to the port side of the mess deck. Just as I was passing near the port ladderway with the hatch above it, I slipped and tossed my tray of food all over the deck behind me. The sea was rough, the ship

---

*Almost 50 years later, in July 1997, my wife Joyce and I took a cruise from Prince Rupert, BC to Ketchikan, and I was amazed at the activity there. Three cruise ships were tied up at the downtown pier, and one was anchored out in the harbor, all at the same time. Now you can probably guess what the main industry is in that town.

was pitching and rolling, and the port hatch leaked water down onto the deck.

The Master-at-Arms was standing right there and said, "You son-of-a-bitch, clean up that mess right now!"

So I cleaned it up and went through the chow line again. As I went through the line, the Master-at-Arms yelled, "Walters, get out of there! You're not going through the line again!"

I replied, "Well, you saw me slip and fall on that wet deck and lose my chow."

He retaliated, "I don't give a damn! I said you went through the line once, and that's all you get!"

For some reason, that 3rd Class bos'n's mate never liked me, because we had had other confrontations before. I could never figure out why.

After noon chow one day, a seaman named Apodaca was playing his guitar, and he was quite good at it, too. Another seaman—I believe it was Willis—grabbed the guitar and framed it around Apodaca's neck. Many of these fellows were foul-ups—I'm not saying those two were— and most had been transferred from other units in the Coast Guard to the *Unalga,* sometimes unaffectionately called the "Dirty U." Over the years I met Coasties from other units who said they had been threatened by their superiors: "If you don't shape up, you could be sent to the *Unalga* for Alaskan duty."

Good heavens, I thought, how or why was I sent on that ship right out of boot camp? Believe it or not, I sort of liked the old ship; she was like a sailor's first girl friend— she kind of broke me in.

In spite of the crew, I thought they were mostly all good guys deep down. They would do anything for one another, and they were loyal. Unfortunately, I can't say much of anything good about the officers.

The *Unalga* was a working ship and worked the islands in the Aleutians. Some crewmen handled the cargo in the ship's hold, others worked on the deck, and a third group was in the beach party that unloaded the LCVPs and carried the supplies through the water and onto the beach. The Aleutian Islands are made of volcanic ash, and every time we took a step, we sank in 6 inches and fell back a foot. Occasionally, we switched jobs.

We arose with the bos'n's pipe at 4 a.m. and worked until 11 p.m., so there were no movies at night. That was okay; we understood that. The food was poor; I really believe the Warrant Commissaryman was trying to save money for the government. Very seldom did we have desserts, like ice cream, which would have been nice once in a while. That would have placated us immensely. There were no night rations at all. Other ships and units throughout the Armed Forces had "night rats" like sandwiches, milk, fresh hot coffee, and fruit like apples and oranges. There was no hot coffee for our workers at night after evening chow about 6 p.m. until morning chow at 5 a.m.

July 1948: One of my *Unalga* shipmates, Heinrich RM3, and I posed on the dock at Ketchikan, Alaska.

The U.S. Navy on Attu offered to give our ship some butter that had been stored there on the island since 1945, three years earlier. Our officers in charge accepted the offer and promptly put all that rancid butter into the general mess for the enlisted men's use. The good, fresh butter we had picked up earlier in Seattle was put into the officers' mess. That was a fact as told to us by the stewards' mates, the officers' messmen. We were told the only way we could get rid of that foul butter was to use it up, so we began to put a half pound on our trays at each meal, then throw it out.

During noon chow, some of the men would check out the deep-sea fishing equipment. After rushing through the noon meal, they would do a little fishing for what little entertainment value there was in it. I think that was the only recreation gear we had aboard.

That went on for a few days; then, suddenly, there was no equipment available, according to the recreation officer. Soon after that, some of the officers showed up on the fantail in the afternoons, fishing with the same gear we had used. The enlisted men from then on were not allowed to fish. All the equipment was divided up and stowed in the officers' staterooms. It eventually went ashore with the officers when we arrived back in Seattle.

On Unimak Island, about 8 miles from Cape Sarichef Light Station, I was working on the shore party, which consisted of one officer and seven men. The ship's radio told us that the weather was going to deteriorate soon and we were to stand by while the ship sought shelter in a cove on Akutan Island.

The last load of supplies had left an hour before for the light station, and we were sure the ship would return soon. We sat on the beach, and we walked the beach, and we waited...and waited. We thought wrong; the ship's radio called back around 8 p.m. and said the ship would not be back until the next morning.

There we were, seven men and one officer sitting on the volcanic beach. No supplies, no water, no shelter, and the ship was saying, "Fend for yourselves, guys." We sat on the beach, we hiked the beach, and we slept on the beach. Luckily it was a fairly warm spring night.

BREAKFAST ON THE BEACH

The ship came back in the morning. They radioed in to us, asking, "Is there anything you'll need on the first boatload we're sending in?"

We all answered in unison: "Yes, send in some breakfast!"

The reply was a simple "Roger."

As the LCVP came up to the beach, a 3rd Class cook stepped ashore and handed the officer a brown paper lunch bag. We were dumbfounded when we looked in the bag; it contained one dozen hard-boiled eggs, 1-1/2 eggs for each of the eight of us.

That predicted storm never came; it was, in fact, a beautiful night, and our mother ship was only 10 or 15 miles away, seeking shelter in a cove! What in heaven's name went through the minds of the CO and the XO, leaving men for whom they were responsible when a storm was supposedly on the way? We had some fine "officers and gentlemen" in our midst!

On July 9th, off Middleton Island in the Gulf of Alaska, we did have a good holiday meal (for the 4th of July, I guess). The menu read: turkey rice soup, roast tom turkey, baked spiced ham, giblet gravy, whipped potatoes...

MESS COOKING

I got one of the better duties of an apprentice seaman when I was assigned as a mess cook for the month of May 1948. A mess cook was paid an extra $16 a month besides his base pay and sea duty pay. I was told that I was to be the mess cook for the CPOs. That meant arising early, right after the cooks, and checking the menu for the day on my way through the ship, then going up to the CPO mess (dining area) and getting the coffee on before anything else. As the chiefs rose and came into the mess, I would tell them what was available for breakfast. I would then go down to the general mess and get the plates of whatever they wanted. Some ate full breakfasts, and some simply wanted only coffee and a cigarette.

When breakfast was over, the chiefs would disperse for their work areas, and I would go into their sleeping quarters and make their racks, sweep the deck, and in general clean up the area and their mess deck. I would then take the dirty dishes down to the scullery, and then, after ensuring that there was more hot coffee brewing, I might get a break.

At noon, I would inform them of what was on the menu, and according to whoever wanted what, I would choose, supposedly, what was the best of the general mess. Afternoons provided a little break, and then it was the same ritual at evening mess for ordering, serving, and clearing away the plates and stainless steel flatware.

I guess that was probably where I learned to drink coffee. I'm not bragging, but the coffee I made in the chiefs' mess was certainly better than that in the general mess. The chiefs might drop in for coffee breaks during the day and insist that I join them. Chief Bos'n Bill Harkens asked me where my home was and where I worked before. I told him that I had worked for Eastman Kodak. After that, I was automatically an expert on cameras and film. I said I'd worked there for only four months, but that didn't matter. He insisted that I tell him what kind of movie camera to buy, a Cine 8 or a 16-mm. How about a beaded screen?

I replied, "I don't know. I never worked with them."

Harkness said, "Well, I want a movie camera. Which is the best?"

Then the chief said, "You must have some idea, seeing you worked at Kodak."

His idea of Kodak must have been a one-room building. I said, "I honestly don't know anything about them, but I suppose I would buy a Kodak."

Harkens said, "Okay, if that's the best, then that's what I'll buy. Now should I get the 16-mm or the Cine 8?"

I mumbled something about the Cine 8 taking twice as much film as the 16mm.

"Chief, you should check out camera shops before you buy."

Later he asked about a 35-mm Automatic Kodak made in those days, and about slides versus prints, etc. Money didn't seem to matter; he just wanted to own some equipment, and he wanted me to tell him what to buy. I figured, what's the use? He couldn't go too far wrong.

Somewhere, someplace, there is someone out there who is—or was—one of the best-equipped amateur photographers in the world—Kodak-equipped, of course.

En route from Ketchikan to Seattle, our ship transmitted, among other things, a radio message stating that Walters, Elmer D., 275-577, Seaman Apprentice, had requested RM (radioman) training. The request was approved, and I was ordered transferred off the "Mighty U." I was told to report on or about Aug. 1, 1948 to the Coast Guard Training Station in Groton, Conn. A few days after that we arrived back at Pier 91 in Seattle.

Shortly after arriving in port, about 20 enlisted men jumped ship for 29 days. Most of them were from the deck force crew. They went AWOL because of the way they had been treated by the officers. I heard about it from a buddy in the group, Al Lentzer, who wrote to me while I was in school.

A hearing was held by the 13th CG District Office in Seattle. When 20 of maybe 70 enlisted men jump ship, there is something drastically wrong. These men returned just short of the time limit for being charged with desertion and were interrogated. Each man told the same story about how they were treated: poor food, no night rations when working 20 hours a day, being cursed at, etc. Of course they had to be found guilty, but they made their point, and it certainly did not look good in the officers' fitness reports, I'm sure. From what I heard, each of the 20 guilty men got about 60 hours of extra duty and was confined to the ship (no liberty) for something like 30 days. They also had to make up for the days they had been "over the hill" at the end of their enlistments.

I was not involved in that situation, because during the last two months in the Aleutians I was allowed to strike for radioman rating. That meant I worked on the deck force in the morning and in the radio room in the afternoon. Three 3rd Class radiomen—Styles, Heinrich (from Iowa), and O'Brien (from California)—were on the ship, and I felt in-debted to them for all the assistance they gave me. They taught me some radio theory, how to make JANAP (radio call signs, etc.) corrections, and—most important—how to make coffee and to keep it always hot.

That was one thing a radioman always had: hot coffee brewing in the radio shack.

VI. REASSIGNMENT

On Aug. 1, 1948, I was en route to Groton from Seattle. I did manage two days at home on the way, and that was the first time I had been back since enlisting.

RADIO OPERATORS' SCHOOL

Radio Operators' School was interesting and enjoyable. Its whole concept of human dignity was different from that of my previous assignment on the *Unalga*. The officers and CPOs who instructed were very sharp and competent. The food was outstanding. For example, at every other Friday night's dinner we were served a *whole lobster.* I had not heard of too many servicemen or ex-GIs who had a *whole lobster* for a meal.

Six months went by rather quickly because I enjoyed school, and the New England area is beautiful, especially in the fall and winter. Weekend liberty in Hartford, Conn., the insurance capital of the world, was great for sailors because there were many young girls working in the insurance offices.

A few of us were known to spend a weekend occasionally in Hartford. Probably once a month I would get a weekend pass, and on Friday at 1600 hours, liberty would be granted. I would take a bus into New London, then catch a New York, New Haven & Hartford train to New York City, arriving about 6:30 p.m. After an hour or two layover, the New York Central train left for Albany, Syracuse, and Rochester and west to Chicago. This was a "milk train," known to make stops at all the jerkwater crossings.

Arriving at Rochester about 6 a.m. Saturday gave me exactly 31 hours at home until I had to leave Sunday for the return to Groton Training Station before the 10 p.m. curfew. The trains ran pretty much on time and I cut my schedule fairly close, but I never had a problem.

Radioman Class #24 was graduated in February 1949. I was 4th in a class of 24 and was immediately sent back to Seattle to await further orders.

While en route from Chicago to Seattle, two CMSTP&P (Chicago, Milwaukee, St. Paul & Pacific) trains were stranded in the Cascade Mountains of eastern Washington. I was on the faster train, the "Olympian Hiawatha," which was blocked by a snowslide. The slower train, the "Columbian Hiawatha," was normally 3 hours behind, but it came up behind us, and shortly thereafter a snowslide occurred and cut off the front of the train from the rear. We were all stranded!

It happened near the Hyack Ski Bowl. Personnel were sent out for help, and later that night a snowplow was on its way to us. The heat was turned down to about 60 degrees to conserve on fuel. Passengers from the slower train were put on our train to save fuel, and we all had to double up, more or less. Everyone had sweaters, jackets, hats, and gloves on, and blankets were passed out as long as they lasted. We ate by candlelight. It was quite cozy, but I suspect that almost everybody would rather have been in Seattle.

The snowplow broke through to us, but then another large slide blocked the snowplow in front of us. After two or three days, arrangements were made for us to walk a short distance to a road, where buses took all of us a few miles to the Great Northern Railroad station in a nearby village, where another train took us to Seattle.

I was listed as AWOL—three days late! When the 13th CGD wanted to know why, I just showed them my "excuse" from the train conductor. Of course, nothing further was said. They assigned me to the Coast Guard base on Denny Way. I had no duties, so they just told me to "hang loose." Reading all the newspapers and magazines and drinking coffee made it quite monotonous. Then, at the end of February 1949, I was given my orders to report to the *CGC Unalga*—again.

Most of the crew were new men, although some were old friends. Leaving in March, we plied the Aleutian Chain and serviced most of the same islands again—Umnak, Unimak, Amchitka, Adak, Attu, and points in between. The biggest difference I noticed about this cruise was that almost all the officers were new. Comdr. Wagline was the CO, and in my book, he was one of the best. He had a very commanding voice; he could stand on the bridge and give orders 300 feet away to someone on the fo'c'sle.

Upon leaving Seattle, we had three radiomen assigned to the ship. A chief radioman was temporarily assigned because he was going to report to the 17th CGD Office in Juneau. There was a 1st Class radioman named Walt Clare who had not been to sea for years and was way past his obligation for sea duty. I was the 3rd Class radioman right out of school.

After we arrived in Alaska, the chief departed, and soon after, 1st Class Radioman Clare flipped out. He sort of went berserk and lost it, threatening to kill the captain in his cabin. The captain held Walt at arm's length and, in his booming voice, commanded him to sit down and not move. The CO then called for the pharmacist's mate, who came running up and gave Walt a sedative. After a discussion, the CO told Walt he would send him back to Seattle ASAP. The CO and Walt agreed it would be best if Walt were locked in the brig out of harm's way.

Capt. Wagline called me to his cabin and informed me of what had happened. He said he realized that I was just out of school, and he asked me if I could handle one-man radio watches. If not, he said, he would take me off watches and just have me operate when there was traffic (radio messages).

I said, "No, sir, I want to operate." I felt I could handle the radio shack alone. I was young and confident and hot to operate as much as I could.

So the CO put me on one-man watches, which meant 0000-0200, 0800-1000, 1200-1400, 1600-1800 hours. Those hours were crazy; I slept maybe 0200 to 0800 (6 hours) and caught an hour or two between 1800 and 0000.

When I was on watch, I would leave the back door of the radio room open and the ET (electronics technician) shop open. Sometimes I would get sick, so I used an old wastebasket for heaving. I finally caught on to what was happening. The diesel fumes from the smokestack would curl down and around the back of the superstructure and roll right in through the back doors to the radio shack. Man, it made some difference when I kept those doors shut.

Before Walt left the ship, I asked the CO if I could see him in the brig. The CO said, "Yes, but check with the pharmacist's mate." I stopped to see Walt, and we talked a few different times after that; it sort of eased his mind about things.

The whole problem was that Walt's wife had threatened to leave him and his two little boys if he went to sea. He had no choice; she knew that when she married a sailor. He had been on shore duty for four to six years, and he was past due for sea duty. His wife gave him an ultimatum, and it worked on his mind. Some time later, I heard that he had gotten out of the service and was pumping gas. His 12 or 13 years of service and his 1st Class rank were all out the window.

I have seen some family men who could handle sea duty or isolated duty for six months or even two years at a time. My philosophy was not to get married as long as I went to sea.

Walt had a Vilbroplex speed key that he wasn't going to need anymore. I had had my eye on it, so I offered to buy it from him. I guess I gave him $15 or $20 for it, and I still have it. It's an antique now.

RAISIN JACK

Nothing much happened through the rest of the voyage except for a couple of noteworthy events. The first was the cook's raisin jack exploding during a Saturday noon inspection. The inspection team consisted of the CO, the XO, the commissary chief, and the yeoman recorder; the cook was standing by.

Then, "WOP!" There was a pause, then "WOP—BOING!"

The captain paused and turned, and the XO and the chief did the same. They looked in the direction of the cabinets in the galley behind the serving line. Then, as they shot a glance at the cook, his eyes rolled up to the overhead, and the captain and the XO kind of smiled, turned, and walked on. The chief at first didn't know what to think, but seeing the captain and the XO moving on, he felt relieved and followed. The yeoman recorder winked at the cook and soon caught up to the party.

The cook was a big burly guy, and he was assigned to do the baking for the cruise, so he would work in the galley around 2 to 4 a.m. I would get off radio watch at 2 a.m., so I'd go down in the galley to shoot the bull with him and have a cup of coffee and maybe try a piece of cake he'd just baked or whatever. He was telling me about the raisin jack episode, and we laughed about it. He could see his stripes going out the window, but the captain was a "real joe."

CRITTER BREAD

One day the cook was kneading bread dough when suddenly the ship rolled, and the dough dropped onto the deck. The area had been fumigated earlier, and there were some dead roaches that ended up in the bread dough when the cook picked it up and put it on the bread board.

I said, "You aren't going to use that now, are you?"

He said, "Sure. No one will know, and it won't hurt them."

I replied, "Well, I know, and I won't eat it."

He countered, "You watch. They'll eat it, and it won't hurt them."

That day at noon chow we had fresh bread, and I actually saw little legs sticking up out of it. No one knew the difference, except me. After that, I was awfully suspicious of all the food for a long time. That cook never offered me any of his raisin jack.

When our ship arrived back in Seattle, I rushed up to the 13th CGD on Second and Marion Streets and took an exam for a speed key certificate. I wanted to be legal in using the "bug" on the circuits (radio frequencies). Chief Radioman Ernie Means administered the exam and gave me my certificate, which made me quite proud. When I returned to the ship, the "Mighty U" was still tied up at Pier 91, Navy Base.

Comdr. Wagline was very instrumental in my being promoted to Radioman 2nd Class in six months because of that voyage. What a difference between the Voyage of 1948 and the Voyage of 1949!

Sometime in November 1949, a message came in stating that the *Unalga* was being decommissioned. I believe the *CGC Storis* was going to replace her in Juneau, Alaska, the 17th CG District. A few days later a message came in from the 13th District transferring me to Seattle Radio Station (NMW) in Westport, Wash., the Primary Radio for the 13th CGD. Besides radio, teletype was tied into all the units along the Coast in the 13th.

VII. ON THE BEACH

The radio station was located about 1.5 miles from the village of Westport, which was and still is a fishing village, and maybe a mile from the Pacific shore, over 100 miles southwest of Seattle, and about 25 miles west of Aberdeen and Hoquiam, a couple of small logging and shipping cities. To the west of the radio station lies a dead-end road that runs for about a mile and ends up at the Pacific shoreline—that is, if the tide is out; if the tide is in, the road is a quarter of a mile shorter.

About 25 to 30 men were assigned to the station under a CO who was a chief warrant radio electrician. A chief radioman named Fryer was the XO of the base. He was a real nice fellow, married with two little kids, and he was to be killed tragically, sometime after I left the base. It seems that he was dating a young divorcée in the area, and they had been out drinking and driving. She was driving and he was hanging out the passenger window. As she sideswiped a telephone pole, his head was smashed, killing him instantly.

Three 1st Class RMs were all married and lived in homes near the base. They were in charge of the three watches. The 3rd Class radiomen, seamen, and the engineering group lived in the main barracks, which had a galley and dining area. The 2nd Class radiomen, including myself, were housed in a small one-story barracks across the street, which had a little more privacy.

When we had liberty, we would walk or ride into the town of Westport, which consisted of two barbershops, two gas stations, two or three bars for sure, and Harry Harm's General Store. Harry had a grocery, meat market, drugstore, soda fountain, and, in the rear, a roller skating rink, all rolled into one conglomeration. Harry was the nicest fellow you would ever want to meet. Almost all of us were too young to drink; even then you had to be 21 to drink in Washington State. We spent most of our time at the soda fountain over a Coke or a cup of coffee. Many of the guys had fake ID cards to show they were older, but I never was tempted to get one.

Around 3 or 4 p.m., the high school bus would stop at Harm's Store and the kids would get off and come in for a Coke. The girls were fascinated by us sailors because we were "men of the world." We had been everywhere and done everything (of course we had), and we had money. Those girls were innocent for the most part, and we would kid with them and maybe buy them a Coke or a soda. We treated them like our kid sisters, and a few of the guys dated the older ones.

One day my buddies asked me to get a date because they were all going to a local high school basketball game that Friday. I asked one of the older-looking girls because someone thought she was 18. She agreed to go, but we had to ride on the school bus, she said. Well, okay, I told my buddies that we would meet them at the game.

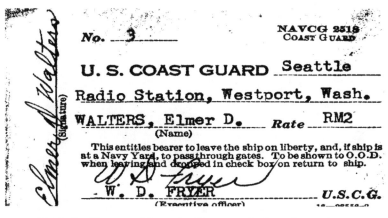

1949: My liberty card from the Westport, Wash. radio station

The game was in Grayland, a town about 10 miles from Westport. During half-time, I asked the girl what class she was in. She said she was a freshman. Then she said she was 15 years old! I was shocked because I didn't know what her folks would think if they knew she was dating a 20-year-old sailor.

One morning as I was standing the 500 Khz watch (International Calling and Distress Frequency), a radioman on a merchant ship was having a hard time trying to transmit a radio message to one of the commercial radio stations, like KFS, KLB, or KSE, for instance, so I offered to relay the message for him.

He was sending rather slowly and deliberately with a hand key, and I answered him with a hand key, telling him to "shift up" to another working frequency. When we acknowledged that we were ready, I told him to go ahead and send his message as I switched to using *my* "bug" (Vibroplex speed key).

This commercial radio officer came back to me with *his* speed key and sent the message so fast that I hardly had time to get my hands on the mill (typewriter).

Was I embarrassed! I had to go back to him and tell him to send the entire message again and to "slow down a bit."

"*Never* send faster than you can receive," was the old adage.

We had been taught that in radio school, but I slipped on that one and thought I was a hot shot. Never again!

Merry Christmas 1949

COMMUNICATIONS SECTION
13TH COAST GUARD DISTRICT

RADM. R. T. MCELLIGOTT..............C13CGD
CAPT. R. J. MAUERMAN..............CH OF STAFF
LT. G. W. SOHM..............CH COMM SECTION
LT J.G. J. L. MITCHELL..............ASST COMM OFFICER

COMMUNICATIONS CENTER 13TH CGD OFFICE

MEANS, E. L...............RMC (LM)
WHITMAN, G. C...............RM1 (GW)
CRAWFORD, T. F...............RM1 (TC)
TOLLERUD, D. A...............RM1 (DA)
FERRELL, A. W...............RM2 (AF)

COMMUNICATIONS TRUCKS

CHRISTMAN, CHARLES E...............RMC (BW)
DENTON, DENNY...............RM1 (DN)
TETTER, JOHN E...............RM1 (JT)
WALKER, KENNETH M...............RM1 (KM)

SEATTLE (WESTPORT) RADIO (NMW)

RELE KENNETH P. HOOD...............OINC (KP)
FRYER, WILLIAM D...............RMC (FR)
RANDALL, SILAS D...............RM1 (SJ)
PEARSON, WOODROW D...............RM1 (PE)
SCHROEDER, ROBERT M...............RM1 (RS)
CASALE, ROBERT...............RM1 (CL)
CHARETTE, ALFRED W...............RM1 (AC)
HARRISON, SHERMAN W...............RM2 (SW)
IRWIN, WALTER L...............RM2 (WI)
WALTERS, ELMER D...............RM2 (EW)
LAHERTY, CHARLES E...............RM2 (CE)
FRANKLIN, JOE L...............SN(RM) (JF)
MAROIS, RENE J...............SN(RM) (MA)
RICHARDS, KENNETH R...............SN(RM) (KR)

ARZADON, LUCAS A...............CS1
McCORD, JAMES S...............BM2
RANKIN, GENE M...............ET3
WALLACE, JAMES E...............EN3
MERINO, JOHN C...............SN
SEIBERLING, DALE G...............SA
KEENEY, JIMMY L...............SA
BERENDT, JAMES L...............SA

and a Happy New Year!
to Mother and Dad,
Elmer

Christmas 1949: Greetings from the Westport, Wash. radio station.

VIII. A HAPPY SHIP

I had been at NMW for about two months when I put in a request for a return to sea duty. The duty at Westport was fine, but it was not for me. I felt I had to have something that gave me more action—a ship to belong to. Westport was isolated duty for me because I preferred a large city to come back to after months at sea.

In March 1950, my request was granted. I was assigned to the *CGC Bering Strait*. I didn't know much about the ship. She was an AVP, small seaplane tender, 311 feet, ex-Navy ship built in 1943, and as I found out later, she had one hell of a war record in the Pacific.

As a radioman, I thought I might be assigned to a 327-foot ship like the *Taney* class or a 250-foot like the *Klamath*. The 327s ride smoothly, and the 250s bob like a cork in the water. The Westport radio station van escorted a few of us up to Seattle and dropped me off, with my seabag, at Haury's Boathouse in West Seattle, across Elliot Bay from Seattle. I took one look at the *Strait* and liked what I saw. She was beautiful, gleaming white with spar trim.

Chief Radioman John Murray introduced himself and welcomed me aboard. I was replacing a fellow named Baker RM2 whose enlistment was up. Baker told me in parting, "You'll love this ship." He was never more right in his life. The other RMs aboard were Bob Alexander RM1, R. E. Morse RM1, Richard Hintz RM3, Bill Godwin RM3, and Mickey Vidaurri SNRM. There were six radio watchstanders and a chief. During April we made one weather patrol, and then I applied for a 30-day leave so I could be home for my 21st birthday in May.

Weather patrol lengths vary because of the time required to cruise to and from the weather station. One weather station, Ocean Station NAN (33° north, 135° west) was between San Francisco and Hawaii. Ocean Station SUGAR (48° north, 162° east) was 125 miles south of the Kamchatka Peninsula of Russia. VICTOR (33° north, 164° east) was east of Guam, and PETER (50° north, 145° west) was more in the center of the North Pacific. Getting to Station SUGAR from Seattle would take probably two weeks, steaming 13 or 14 knots in those days. That was taking the Great Circle Route, which meant that going in a straight line, the ship would head up through the Aleutian Islands, past Attu and Shemya Islands, and down past the Russian waters to north of Japan.

My previous leave had been in February 1949—12 days after graduating from radio school. Before I took the 1950 leave, an ALCOAST bulletin, known throughout the service as "gospel truth," came out stating that anyone who had enlisted for a four-year term could be discharged after three years. That meant I would be getting out in December 1950, a year earlier than I had expected. Going home, I was very excited about getting out early, but I also had some reservations about leaving theCoast Guard life. However, after enjoying my family and friends and tipping a few with my old hometown buddies, I was ready to go back to my ship and Seattle.

1950: The *CGC Bering Strait* in the Straits of Juan de Fuca en route to Seattle.

Soon after we went to sea for another weather patrol, Ocean Station NAN (33° north, 135° west), the Korean War started in late June 1950. All early discharges were canceled, and our enlistments were, in fact, extended for the duration of the war.

When I went home in May, I stopped to see John Murray's very Italian mother, who lived in Buffalo. John's father was Irish. His mother insisted that I take some goodies to give to him. She was a very nice lady, and I was more than glad to do it. When I arrived back in Seattle, John insisted that I come to his home for dinner and meet his family. He had a strikingly beautiful brunette wife and a 9-year-old boy. An Italian dinner was served, I remember, and they kept prodding me to eat more. I get filled up easily on pasta, but their son ate three times as much as I did.

Chief Murray made two more patrols after I had first come aboard, then was transferred to Westport to replace Chief Fryer, who had been killed in that auto accident.

Chief Ernie Means from the 13th CGD called me at that time to tell me he was coming onto the *Strait*. He wanted me to watch for some of his gear that he was sending ahead. We had met earlier in the Radio Division in the 13th District Office, and we were to become good friends. Years later, maybe in the late '50s, I heard from an old buddy that Ernie had died an alcoholic.

Comdr. Morell was the CO on the *Strait*. Lt. Comdr. R. D. Brodie 4th was the XO.

Every day we had drills, usually at 1300 after the noon chow. One of the drills we practiced was GQ (General Quarters). "All hands to Battle Stations!" was the PA message, and the klaxon horn would blow over and over. Everyone would run to his assigned station; I rushed up to the very top of the superstructure to man the MK57 Director. I had to put a belt around my waist so I could swing the big director around to 360 degrees on a platform and hang onto the arms to direct it on a vertical plane. Sighting through magnified crosshairs, I could see objects thousands of feet away. The Director was tied in with the 5-in. gun mount on the forward main deck. This was mostly for firing at an airborne target.

At my GQ station, many times when we were tied up at Haury's Boathouse in West Seattle, we would have one of these drills. The gunnery officer would say, "Walters, pick a target and track it."

"Yes, sir."

Some unsuspecting person would be driving along the West Seattle road passing Haury's Boathouse. Quite often he would glance at our ship, then do a "double-take" as he noticed a big gun barrel pointed right at him and tracking him down the road. I could always see the driver in my gun sight, and he often looked a little perplexed.

In October 1950, our ship went to Bremerton Shipyards to have K-guns, Y-guns, and depth charge racks installed on the fantail. We crossed Puget Sound from Seattle to Bremerton on the Black Ball Ferry Lines. The famous *Kalakala* was an ultrastreamlined ferry, but I think it had more rattles than any other two ferryboats combined.

We pulled most of our liberty in Seattle. That meant catching a ferry at Bremerton at about 5 p.m. and getting into Seattle around 6 p.m. If a sailor had a date, he didn't pick her up until maybe 7 p.m. The last ferry at night ran at maybe 1:30 or 2 a.m. from the ferry docks in Seattle, so his goodnight kiss had to be delivered before that. If he missed the last ferry, he had to stay at the Servicemen's YMCA and catch the early ferry in the morning, before 0745 muster.

FALL 1950

The shipyard had a "gedunk" about halfway between the main gate and where the *Strait* was anchored. Around mid-morning, two or three of us would go over for coffee and fraternize with a couple of girls who worked there. Near Halloween time, I yelled, "Trick or treat!" and they gave us each a donut with our coffee, which was a pleasant surprise. After that, one of the girls always kept me in donuts free of charge. I guess I was too naïve to figure it out.

One time, my buddy and I came across on the ferry from Seattle to Bremerton late at night. We had had a few beers, and after the ferry docked, we hailed a cab for the shipyard. The cabbie took off roaring up the street and—WHAM!—BAM!—drove right into a Bremerton police car parked alongside the curb.

The cabbie said, "Jesus! I must have dozed off!"

Dozed off? He must have been sound asleep! We weren't hurt, but that cruiser sure was smashed.

The officers had just gotten out of the cruiser and were going into an all-night diner. They whirled around and in a flash had that cabbie out of his cab and against its door.

My buddy and I climbed out of the cab and decided to get a cup of coffee in the diner. A few minutes later we finished our coffee and called another cab. As we left for the shipyard in the second cab, the two officers still had that cabbie under questioning near his hack.

My buddy and I laughed about it later. When that cabbie first picked us up and started roaring down the street, I thought something was funny. We had to be doing 25 or 30 mph when we sideswiped the police car.

In early November, Bill Godwin wanted me to go with him down to Salem, Ore. to visit some friends of his family from Iowa. It was on a Saturday that we took a Greyhound bus to Salem; we traveled all day, and I was dead tired. His friends met us at the bus station, and we drove about 20 miles. We stood around talking, and I could hardly stay awake.

After dinner, they all talked and talked, and then they decided to show home movies of everyone back home in Iowa. It was so hot in the kitchen where we were watching the movies that I decided to stand up near the door where it might be a little cooler. The next thing I remember, I actually dozed off, standing up!

Finally the movies ended, and they showed Bill and me to our rooms. I had never enjoyed lying down in a bed so much in my whole life as I did that night. But we had a good time, and I'm sure Bill enjoyed it.

The radio watches were set up this way: Bob Alexander RM1 and Bill Godwin RM3, R. E. Morse RM1 and Dick Hintz RM3, and Elmer ("Walt") Walters RM2 and Billy Howell RM3. Almost everyone was happy with the setup. I think Alex and Bill had the middle watches (0000 to 0400 and 1200 to 1600), then Morse and Dick had 0400 to 0800 and 1600 to 2000. Billy and I had 0800 to 1200 and 2000 to 2400. Chief Means would copy press for the latest news to put into a ship newsletter. Quite often the chief would ask me to copy the PRESS. It was a high-speed code of 30 to 40 words per minute.

Most of the ship's business was conducted by radio during the 0800-1200 watch. The ship carried four or five Civil Service meteorologists aboard, and after they interpreted the weather, we would send coded messages back to the States. All three watches transmitted weather reports every day at sea.

1950-52

The meteorologists sent balloons, called "rawins,"* to the upper atmosphere. A small package on the balloon contained a radio transmitter that sent data back to the weather shack. The meteorologists would then bring us radiomen the coded messages, which we would transmit to the San Francisco Navy radio.

The messages were all numbers in groups of five, such as 12345 54321 55555 00000. Using a speed key, an operator could really rip off a message in a short time. Even with the use of a hand key, the messages went quite rapidly. We used shortcuts whenever we could; for example, a 5 is five dits†, but when we had five 5s, we sent one dit for each 5. Then with a little longer spacing in between, we sent only five dits for 55555. For a zero, instead of five dashes, we transmitted one dash held a little longer than normal, so a series of 00000 made only five dashes. All this saved a lot of time, and with a good operator receiving on the other end, we got a "Roger" back in a short time.

NOON SOUP

Mess cooks are usually junior seamen who serve one month a year assisting the cooks. They set out the tables and condiments and serve on the steam line, then they clear the mess deck. Vidaurri had asked to be transferred from the radio gang (0 Division) to the Deck Division, and now he was mess-cooking.

----

*Rawinsonde: a radiosonde tracked by a radio direction-finding device to determine the velocity of winds aloft.
Radiosonde: a miniature radio transmitter carried aloft, as by an unmanned balloon, with instruments for broadcasting, by means of precise tone signals, the humidity, temperature, and air pressure.

†Dit: a dot in radio or telegraphic code.

One of the minor but essential duties of an XO on a naval ship is to sample the daily noon meal that is served to the crew.

This one episode occurred when the XO, Lt. Comdr. R. D. Brodie 4th, a very haughty and arrogant individual, began sampling the food behind the serving line. The weather happened to be quite rough, and the ship was encountering some large swells, maybe 25 to 30 degrees. At that time, Vidaurri had just taken a large metal container, maybe 5 gallons of soup, out of the dumbwaiter to lift up to the steam line. The container spilled, Vidaurri slipped, and everything hit the deck.

At that moment, the ship rolled to port; the soup, mess cook, and container came swooping down the deck, knocking Brodie 4th off his feet. The whole mishmash went sliding across the mess deck, then back across to starboard. The XO was sliding flat on his back in the soup, cursing and swearing at Vidaurri, who was having a ball, laughing and rolling around, knowing it was almost impossible to stand up. He was trying to hold onto that 5-gallon container so it wouldn't smash into the XO.

After a few round trips, the XO and the mess cook managed to get on their feet. The XO went stomping off to "Officers' Country" wearing his new decorations of corn, beans, peas, and maybe some beef parts. Vidaurri and everyone else who saw it laughed a million laughs. The crew standing in line for early watchstanders' chow certainly had a ringside seat.

HOLIDAY SEASON, 1950

In 1950, Thanksgiving was celebrated early on ship because the *Bering Strait* was being assigned to the new Ocean Station SUGAR, about 125 miles southeast of the Kamchatka Peninsula in Russia. The ship had a huge Thanksgiving dinner for all hands, including their wives, families, and sweethearts. My buddies and I invited our girl friends over for the dinner, and tours were allowed throughout the ship, except below deck.

A couple of my buddies (at least I thought they were) kept ribbing me about showing my girl friend, Betty, the "Golden Rivet" on the ship. I was very embarrassed and tried to play it down. Finally Betty overheard and, in a young girl's innocence, kept after me to show her the "Golden Rivet." Some of the old-timers overheard with their wives, and days later they were still razzing me: "Hey, Sparks, have you shown that cute girl the 'Golden Rivet' yet?"

After saying all our good-byes, a couple of days later we departed from Seattle for Station SUGAR via the Great Circle Route.

As we neared the Aleutians, we began picking up many different radio calls in the Far East. There were Japanese, Russian, Dutch, English, and other nationality call signs. While on watch, I picked up three SOSs at one time from ships in distress. Their positions indicated they were 800 to 1,000 miles away (radio signals carry much farther at night than during the day).

A universal radio rule of the sea states that as soon as distress calls are intercepted, all other radio traffic must cease immediately to allow the distressed traffic to continue unimpeded. Despite this regulation, the Russians would invariably get on the air and interfere. They tuned their radio transmitters back and forth across 500 Kcs (kiloherz), the International Calling & Distress Frequency. Russian ships would call RHH, the main Vladivostok radio station that handled Russian traffic in that area of the Pacific, over and over by the hour. I firmly believed they deliberately tried to disrupt any distressed vessels that were not their own.

We could always tell Russian ship signals because they sounded like the old "spark gap" transmitters used before World War II. Their signals sounded like hens cackling.

I did get back at them. One night, a Russian ship that always called constantly, the *UOVY,* kept calling RHH hour after hour. I flipped on my 500-watt TAJ Model low-frequency transmitter and sent "Dah-dit-dah," the code for the letter K, which means, "Go ahead, send your message."

Well, that ship went ripping through her message and waited, and waited—and waited. There was no "Roger" from RHH because he must have been out to lunch. Finally, the *UOVY* was able to raise RHH and had to send her traffic all over again, hours later.

The Coast Guard always monitored the International Calling & Distress Frequencies: 500 Kcs (low frequency), 8270 Kcs (high frequency), and 220.5 Mcs (very high frequency). All these frequencies were monitored faithfully by all ships and stations that had radio watchstanders.

The other operator on the two-man watch would be devoted to Coast Guard traffic, listening on 22.5 Mcs and monitoring the Ocean Station beacon. When we arrived on station, we would transmit a radio beacon signal, continuously, such as 4YN (Station NAN) or 4YS for Station SUGAR.

NUD, Navy Radio Adak, could be heard for many miles. Passing through that area was like old home week to me because I had cruised the Aleutians for almost two years aboard the *Unalga.* I had worked NUD from the *Unalga,* whose call was NRCP. Some Navy operators were not regarded as the best at operating because they usually did only one thing or the other, sending or receiving. The Coast Guard, a much smaller outfit, trained its operators to be highly proficient, not only in sending and receiving but also in teletype operation and in maintenance and repairs.

This was especially true aboard ship where, on many units, there were no electronic technicians. The Coast Guard was also known, at one time in the late '40s, to have a high-speed code circuit between Alaska and the States. One thing an operator had to remember was never to transmit faster than he could receive, because the rate at which he transmitted a message determined how fast the other operator would send his message back.

However, as we passed through that area of the North Pacific, NUD could be heard nightly sending CQs on the International Calling & Distress Frequency (500 Kcs) incessantly. They sounded as if they were trying to drum up traffic to overcome a dull mid-watch. That type of operation was frowned upon by military communications.

Six or eight months later, when the *Strait* was back in Seattle, I happened to walk into the Maison Blanche, a fairly discreet restaurant, to meet a couple of my shipmates. Bert St. Romain, ET3, and Billy Howell, RM3, called me over.

"Walt, come here; we have someone we want you to meet!"

I said I didn't believe I knew the fellow who greeted me. He was a Navy radioman who had been stationed at NUD for past two years.

It seemed that he had known it was I who was on watch and working the Navy on the radio circuits as the *Strait* was cruising past Adak. He said he recognized my "fist" (hand key") over the years.*

"It's truly a small world!" I said.

Ocean Station SUGAR is strategically located where weather fronts blowing across the North Pacific originate. Main airline routes between the United States and Japan were utilized by us with our radio beacon and radar. Northwest Airlines, for instance, flew this Great Circle Route from Seattle to Tokyo. We were often told that we were a comforting factor, sometimes in the middle of the night, to those sky crews as they passed overhead. Some of the fellows in Radar, behind the bridge, talked to the pilots and even the stewardesses at times. A good friend of mine from New Orleans (he always pronounced it "Norlans") dated one of the Northwest stewardesses. Bert and Bernice made a cute couple around Seattle when we were in port and she was between flights.

Our first tour of SUGAR was coming to an end in December, and we awaited our relief, the *CGC Minnetonka*. She was out of Long Beach, Calif. and had a record of not relieving us on time. The crew of the *"Minnie"* did drop us a Christmas tree they had brought out, which was greatly appreciated. We set it up on our mess deck.

Leaving the *Minnetonka* to her duties, we departed straight for Japan and the excitement of the Far East.

Ten or 12 days before Christmas, our ship tied up in Yokosuka, Japan, and we entered a different world. Japan had come a long way since the end of the war in 1945. They had rebuilt, and areas were cleaned up pretty much, but the people were poor. They made use of all the

---

*A radioman using Morse Code leaves an indelible print that can be recognized by a fellow operator. The way he transmits is similar to his handwriting or his voice. Therefore, if an operator hears a fellow operator enough times, he is going to recognize that operator. Even so, it was amazing to have met that Navy man who recognized my "fist"!

garbage off our ships and bases, and I don't think it was only for their livestock.

The monetary rate was 360 yen to the American $1. American servicemen were known to be quite affluent.

The *Strait* tied up at the Yokosuka Naval Base. Before going ashore, we had to exchange American dollars for military scrip, then on shore exchange the scrip for yen on the base before going into the Japanese market.

Prices on items were very reasonable in 1950, such as a kimono for 1,000 yen ($2.77). I guess we all had a heyday buying souvenirs for everyone back home. Some fellows bought complete sets of Noritake china. I bought my mother a set. I also bought some silk paintings depicting the Japanese scenes of Mt. Fuji. Some of those paintings turned out to be rare and valuable.

Arrangements were made for 20 or 25 of the crew to go to an Army-operated rest camp in Yamanaka, located near Shimoyoshida, a small village at the foot of Mt. Fuji. We took a train for two or three hours, I remember, and crowded into an old passenger car with wooden seats in the back. It was so packed with the natives that all our group stood up for the entire trip. Vendors came alongside the train at all stops to sell packaged food. I was daring, so I purchased a package of dried squid. I tried to chew on that squid but finally gave up after an hour. Some of the guys tried smoked oysters, but I couldn't stand the smell of them.

During the few days we had been in the country, we had picked up some Japanese music and records. As our train clickety-clacked through the countryside, the crowd started singing a popular song called "China Night." We sailors sang our version to the tune of what we thought the other people were singing: "She ain't got no yo-yo, she ain't got no yo-do-ooohh." My favorite was "Kan-Kan Musume," a song about a poor Japanese girl standing on the street corner of the Ginza and describing how she was dressed, just waiting for her boy friend to meet her. Both were beautiful songs.

It was early evening when we arrived at the Yamanaka Hotel. We were divided into groups of four to a room. My buddy Billy Howell and I were odd men out, so we had an American-style room to ourselves. American-style meant regular beds, chairs, solid walls, and a door. The others had Japanese paper walls and paper sliding doors, blankets on the floor for beds, and no chairs. It seemed as if Billy and I entertained the troops in our room most of the time.

Every morning after breakfast, most of us went horseback riding. The Japanese in the area would bring their horses (horses? Some of the animals had fur!) to rent to us by the hour or day. I would usually ride all morning with an engineman named Williams from North Carolina. Once we rode almost up to a tree line and into a canyon that kept getting narrower and narrower until we had to tether off the horses at a bush. Then we climbed up a hill, and on top was a pillbox. This evidence was proof positive that the Japanese had intended to fight to the bitter end, probably all the way up to the peak of Mt. Fuji.

I took pictures of the scene; then we left to return to the camp. Arriving back at the hotel, we found most of our buddies sipping beer in the fireside lounge where they had been camping since breakfast.

1950: E. L. Williams EN3 (left) and I riding up the slopes of Mount Fuji.

One night a geisha party was arranged for us. We sat cross-legged on the floor with shoes off at a small table about 10 in. high, four to a table. The geishas (professional dancers) knelt on the floor, and one would serve maybe three or four tables. They stir-fried the sukiyaki and kept our little sake* containers constantly full. Beer was served with everything, and it made quite an interesting banquet. Occasionally the geishas would go up front and sing and dance to the accompaniment of stringed instruments.

Five days went by quickly, and we sadly checked out to return to Yokosuka. Upon arriving back at the *Strait,* we were able to celebrate Christmas and have a huge party for some Japanese war orphans on the ship. Each child was given a large paper bag with all kinds of penny candy, popcorn, and a toy in it. They were shown some American cartoons, then treated to a turkey dinner with all the trimmings. Needless to say, they didn't eat it. They would have preferred rice and fish.

After three weeks of RRR (rest, recreation, and refueling), we shoved off to return to Ocean Station SUGAR for another month.

Christmas 1950: I sent my folks this card from the *CGC Bering Strait.*

---

*A rice wine.

JANUARY 1951: SUGAR PATROL

Nothing much of importance transpired during the January '51 SUGAR patrol. The *Strait* returned in mid-February and tied up at Haury's Boathouse in West Seattle. Shortly after, we went into dry-dock at Todd Shipyard. Repairs were made to the ship after three wintry months of patrol in the North Pacific.

The *Bering Strait,* WAVP-382, was built in 1943 in Houghton, Wash. She displaced 2800 tons and was 311 feet long and 41 feet 2 in. at her broadest beam. She had a 13-foot draft. Propulsion machinery was four 1600-hp diesel engines, twin screw. We cruised at about 11 to 13 knots, not very fast compared with today's ships. Our complement was about 100 men and 10 officers.

Before obtaining permission from the OOD, I went down onto the dry-dock floor to inspect the Sonar dome, forward under the hull. It was quite a sensation to be standing underneath the whole ship, which was up on blocks, entirely out of the water.

February 1951: Beneath the hull of the *Bering Strait* in Todd Shipyard. To my right on the floor is a Sonar dome.

In March we were headed south to San Diego for gunnery range practice. Usually two ships traveled together, so the *CGC Winona,* homeported in Port Angeles, joined us as we cruised down the West Coast. We had daily drills at 1300, either surface fire practice or antiaircraft fire. For the latter, the meteorologists would release a balloon, and after a few minutes, when the balloon had attained sufficient altitude, the Fire Control Command would direct me to track the balloon, and at his command I would "fire" from the MK57 Director that was located at the very top of the superstructure. The 5-in. gun mount on the main deck was tied in directly to the MK57 Director, and whichever way I aimed my sights, the 5-in. rifle would fire.

February 1951: My General Quarters (Battle) Station, MK57 (Fire Control) Director

Every two years, as two ships paired up for the gunnery practice, there was a little rivalry between the crews. In San Diego, the crews on liberty would meet, and the losers had to buy the beer for the winners. Two years before, the *Winona* had won the contest, but this year, we on the *Strait* felt confident.

When we entered the range, the *Winona* went first during the morning session, and the *Strait* followed, awaiting her turn in the afternoon. The Navy tug pulled a barge with a large screen that simulated a ship; they were maybe 5 to 8 miles away. As we observed the *Winona,* she dropped her first shot thousands of yards short. The next shot was even shorter, but as she corrected her elevation, the third shot went over the horizon. We were baffled, but we learned later that they had problems with their sound-powered phones throughout the ship.

My GQ station for surface fire was at Fire Control, located just forward of the superstructure, above the bridge. My assignment was to operate a World War II Eastman Kodak wind-up computer, Model Mark 57. Mr. Getz was the Fire Control officer, and the third man at the station was my good buddy, Johnny Johnson RD3, who was the telephone talker.

I would activate the computer by winding it up like a clock with a key. Then, given my True Course and True Speed, I would then estimate the target's course (relative to us), speed, and distance in yards.

IX. ELEVEN OUT OF TWELVE

As Radar Control gave me the target's exact range and speed, I would make fine adjustments to the computer, and when everything clicked off in unison, I knew my parameters were right on target. I called out the parameters to Johnny and he, in turn, repeated them over the sound-powered phones to the 5-in. gun mount. With azimuth and elevation, plus windage, added in, the Fire Control officer would give the order to "Fire!" and Johnny would pass the word to the gun crew.

That year the *CGC Bering Strait* fired 11 shots—*directly through the screen*—and the 12th shot was close enough to be a hit if the target had been a real ship. The Navy said it was some of the best firing they had ever seen at the San Diego range. That was really something, for the Navy to acknowledge that about the Coast Guard gunnery. I felt quite proud about it because I had set up the surface fire problem initially. Observing those results made me feel great.

A happy time was had by all the *Strait* crew on liberty that evening in ol' San Diego. We had vindicated ourselves over the *Winona* crew.

In April, Billy Howell and I took a 12-day leave to spend in Long Beach, Calif. We had a ball, enjoying ourselves visiting with a couple of girls we had met earlier when our ship visited Long Beach on the way back from San Diego to Seattle. Billy and I stayed at the Servicemen's YMCA in Long Beach and spent time at the Plunge, a large indoor public swimming pool, long since gone. We also enjoyed the large amusement park right on the beach, called the Pike, where there was a roller coaster that went out over the ocean. That was quite a thrill!

Later in August 1951, I met someone who was to change my life forever. One night, in the ship's "hangout" (every ship's crew has its own bar, and ours was the Drift Inn on 5th Avenue in Seattle), I met a girl who had come in with a couple of her girl friends, who called her "Irish." I asked her to dance, and I guess I asked her for every dance after that. I asked Irish if she would like to see a movie the next night, and she agreed.

But I had forgotten that I was supposed to go to another girl's (Joan's) house for dinner that same night. Joan, whom I had met maybe a year earlier, was as cute "as a bug in a rug." We had dated occasionally. Then, believe it or not, I had made another date for the very same night with a girl whom my friend, Chief Ernie Means, had introduced me to just a few nights before. So there I was with three different dates for the same night.

Having known Joan for some time, I went to her house for dinner. She lived with her mother on one of the houseboats that used to be on Lake Washington. After a little wine and a good dinner, I begged off and left early. I had completely forgotten about the third girl.

I hurried to pick up Irish for the movie. She was the most alluring and attractive girl I had ever met. I was completely captivated by her.

Irish was a third-year law student, staying with old friends and working for the summer in Seattle. After that night we dated steadily, except for the better part of September, when the *Strait* went to Station NAN for weather patrol.

FALL 1951

Irish and I promised to write to each other every day. The only time that letters could be exchanged at sea was when the ship that we relieved took our mail back to port, or the ship that relieved us brought our mail to us. That gave us a week or 10 days before we would be back in port.

Ocean Station NAN was located between San Francisco and maybe two-thirds of the way to Hawaii. The weather was great at that time of year, so some of the crew would work out on deck, usually after the daily drills. With a couple of hours of spare time until evening chow, some would do calisthenics or lift weights in the weight room.

One of my best friends, Johnny Johnson from Minnesota, had come aboard the *Strait* in September 1950. He was a physical education graduate, 6 feet tall, 175 pounds, and all muscle without an ounce of fat. He had a 32-in. waist and a 35-in. reach. We still visit and write occasionally, although we live 2,000 miles apart. To this day, now in his 70s, Johnny is still in excellent shape.

In contrast, although I, too, am 6 feet tall, I have only a 33-in. reach and never weighed more than 165 pounds.

After our warm-ups on the ship, including skipping rope, we would wrap our fists, then use the speed bag and punch the heavy bag. We worked on those for 15 minutes, then took a 5-min. break.

Johnny would say, "Okay, Walt, let's box a couple rounds."

He was not only a good amateur boxer but also an excellent trainer and instructor. We put on headgear to protect our ears, mostly. Johnny used to "toy" with me, but I enjoyed the challenge. I know I got plenty of exercise bobbing and weaving from his flurries. Sometimes he would nail me good, decking me once and almost knocking me over the side of the ship. Only once did I feel that I got the best of him for a short time because he cut easily, and his lips were cut enough to stop our sparring.

One day a fellow named Gabriel, about 5 feet, 10 in. and maybe 170 pounds, came around and told how he used to fight in "smokers" in the 11th Coast Guard District (Los Angeles). He wanted to work out with us, and after a few days Johnny asked Gabe if he wanted to go a couple of rounds with one of us.

Gabe said, "Sure, but we never wore headgear like you guys do."

Johnny replied, "We wear all the protection we can get. It protects your ears, for one thing."

Gabe mocked the use of headgear. We used 6-ounce gloves, so I wrapped Gabe's fists and put his mitts on him.

Gabe said, "Okay, let's go."

Johnny took his stance, threw a left jab, right cross, a left hook, and a right uppercut.

Gabe never got in a punch as he doubled over and fell back. He yelled, "That's enough! Jesus Christ, you guys play hard!"

He ripped off his headgear, and I rushed over to help him get his mitts off.

Johnny was still dancing around and hadn't even worked up a sweat. He asked, "What's with that guy?"

I said, "I think you hurt his feelings. He expected a dance."

Gabe walked away slowly and a little uneasily. He never again came up on deck during our workouts.

Boxing was not foremost with us; rather it was the fresh air and exercise we got that were more important. I knew that some of my buddies would rather lie in their sacks and sleep away their free time than work up a sweat.

Johnny had boxed a fellow once, back in Minnesota, who later fought Chuck Davey, a good, clever fighter who appeared on TV on the *Pabst Blue Ribbon Wednesday Night Fights*. Davey ended up meeting his "Waterloo" when Kid Gavilan, with the "Bolo Punch," trounced him soundly.

When I returned from patrol, Irish and I saw a lot of each other. Near the end of September she was preparing to leave for school in Montana. We talked at length about our futures and a future together. We decided that she would finish law school and get her degree first. I could only make plans after getting out of the Coast Guard. My future was indefinite because all enlistments were frozen for the duration of the Korean War. I did have some thoughts about wanting to continue in radio as a radio officer in the Merchant Marine, if I could get a ship. I realized that I would never get married as long as I went to sea, so I wanted to sail only for a couple of years.

In late October, I applied for 30 days' leave to spend a week visiting Irish, then going to New York for the remainder of my leave. The *Strait* was making preparations to leave for the Far East SUGAR patrol in December.

As things turned out, Irish and I came to a parting of the ways, not knowing exactly what happened. I do know that my strict upbringing and foolhardy stubbornness made me regret many things for the rest of my life.

Webster's Dictionary defines *obstinate* as "1: perversely adhering to an opinion, purpose, or course in spite of reason, arguments, or persuasion; 2: not easily subdued..." That definition fit me to a T, and not being very mature, I assumed there was always time in the future to make amends.

There was a Door to which I found no key:
There was a Veil past which I could not see:
Some little Talk awhile of Me and Thee
There seemed—and then no more of Thee and Me.

—Rubaiyat of Omar Khayyam

I continued traveling home to Hilton, where I visited with my family and friends for 10 or 12 days, not really caring about anything. Eventually I told my mother that I had to return to my ship early. She thought I had planned to spend the rest of my leave at home. I told her my plans had been changed and that I had to get back to Seattle. Little did she know that I really didn't give a damn about anything from then on. We were never a family that could talk things out and share our feelings or problems. It just wasn't done in my family.

DECEMBER 1951

The *Strait* had had a new skipper for the past few months—Comdr. J. E. Richey, an excellent officer and well liked by everyone.

We shoved off in December for the second year of SUGAR patrols in the Far East, with some veterans of the preceding year and some new men on board. The radio gang was a little different: Morse RM1 was discharged after more than 20 years and went back, I presume, to his home state of North Carolina. Bob Alexander RM1 and Bill Godwin RM3 had the first section. Barnes RM2, who had been assigned just before SUGAR, and Billy Howell RM3 had the second section. John Barrett RM3 and I had the third section.

Barrett had come aboard in the fall. He was from Auburn, Wash., where his wife and little girl lived. I remember him saying that his father, in the U.S. Navy, had been killed in a submarine during World War II.

One cloudy but clear afternoon, just before being relieved from our station, we had a little excitement.

"Plane overhead!" the PA system blared out, and everyone not on watch poured out of the hatches to watch on deck.

I believe it was an Air Force B-17 that did a flyover, maybe 150 to 200 feet above sea level, sweeping past the port side, bow to stern, about 300 feet horizontally. It flew out of Adak to drop us a real live 6-foot Christmas tree (it must have come from the mainland) and a waterproof bag of paperback books and magazines. The aircraft circled again, then flew on to Japan

A boat coxswain, an engineer, and a couple of seamen were lowered over the side in our power lifeboat to retrieve the tree and bag. That was quite thrilling, seeing a big plane coming in so low and sweeping by, and it was comforting to know that someone else from home came by to say "Hello."

Returning to Japan for two weeks for R&R was once more very interesting. Although we did not go to the Yamanaka Hotel & Rest Camp near Shimoyoshida, we saw more sights around Tokyo. We also visited the Yokohama area and Kamakura. The Dai-Butsu Buddha was very interesting to see in Kamakura, as were many of the Shinto shrines located there.

We bought the usual souvenirs again, although I did have a rather unusual request from my brother-in-law. He wanted a couple of postage stamps that Japan had just issued the preceding month. I went to a post office in Yokosuka and tried to get across to the clerk that I wanted a block of four stamps, like the newspaper clipping I showed him. He motioned for me to go to the door on the right, and he unlocked it and motioned for me to come in. It looked like any old-time post office to me. He led me over to an old rolltop desk, pulled up a swivel chair for me, and pulled out some pigeon-hole drawers and motioned for me to "go at it."

I sat down in amazement and thought to myself, why not get two stamps of every kind and a couple of sheets of the commemorative stamps that my brother-in-law wanted? I probably sat there for a half-hour going through everything, and I really enjoyed it.

When I finished, I arose and said, "A-ree-a-too!" ("Thank you!").

The clerk bowed and said he was pleased to have served me.

I don't remember exactly how many different kinds of stamps I bought, but even counting the sheets of the new commemoratives, they couldn't have cost over a few hundred yen. I wrapped the stamps in waxed paper and mailed them in a tube to my brother-in-law. At that moment I wished I had an interest in collecting or had even purchased some sheets for myself. They increased in value immensely over the next 10 to 15 years.

NEW YEAR'S EVE, 1951

On New Year's Eve, a few of us took a train to Yokohama. We had a good dinner at an Allied Personnel Restaurant, and mine cost 68 cents. The main street where the restaurant was located was called Isezaki-cho.

My shipmates and I entered a so-called nightclub that featured some Japanese hostesses for dancing, what we used to call taxi dancers in the States. They wore American-style formal gowns. There was an old pot-bellied stove off to the side of the dance floor, and the girls gathered around the stove to keep warm between dances. Suddenly a couple of the girls pulled up their long skirts to get warmer, and—lo and behold!—they had U.S. Army khaki wool "long johns" (GI underwear) on underneath. It was enough to turn a few sailors off, and we finished our beers and left.

We hailed a Japanese taxicab to take us back to Yokosuka Naval Base. That cab ride was by far the most breathtaking automobile ride I had had in a long time. We roared down the street, dodging other cars on either side, barely missing pedestrians, and swerving around potholes and mud puddles when the cabbie could see them. Between Yokohama and Yokosuka, we raced along next to a train for a long way, and ahead we could see that we were going to intersect with that train shortly. On the edge of our seats, we watched anxiously; we couldn't convey our anxiety to the cabbie, who was very limited in English and common sense. In a few seconds we made a sharp left oblique turn and went careening over the tracks *just* ahead of the train.

We ended the night at the Enlisted Men's Club having a few more beers as we watched a group of Marines fighting among themselves. It all started when a sailor decked a Marine, so the Marine's buddy started beating on the first Marine for losing a fight to a "swabbie." Then others jumped in, taking sides.

The three of us "Coasties," still shaking from the excitement of that cab ride, just sat there in our booth and ducked as beer was thrown all around our area. Then some Marines jumped over our booth trying to get to the other Marines (we helped boost a few over) as we tried to protect our beer. No sailors, Navy or Coast Guard, were bothered as those Marines went at one another.

The Shore Patrol broke it up in a short time, and everyone went back to drinking with their buddies again. I remember the Japanese female vocalists were singing country/Western songs. They loved our American music, especially Western.

OCEAN STATION VICTOR

Leaving Yokosuka early in January 1952, we cruised down to a new weather station, VICTOR, situated halfway between Japan and Guam. The exact location was 33 degrees north latitude and 164 degrees east longitude.

Every day on patrol there were drills of some kind or other. If there was inclement weather, we would have classes, maybe for the entire crew, or each division would have its own classes. Classes for the O division would be in semaphore or flashing light, taught by the quartermasters, and the radiomen would join in. Radiomen were usually pretty good at flashing light, but our problem was that we had a tendency to send messages too fast. You can't read flashing light anywhere near as fast as you can hear audible sounds.

During fair weather, every drill would be conducted topside (on deck). The weather on VICTOR was very pleasant, around 60 to 70 degrees, not requiring foul weather jackets for most of the time.

General quarters was held often, but one day we tried to practice antiaircraft gunnery with our 5-in. gun. I controlled the gun mount from the Director 57 Gun Control Station. We hadn't fired the gun since it was smashed by a storm the preceding November. The first time I tried, nothing happened. We finally got the problem fixed—it was in the wiring—and fired four or five shots at the target.

The Fire Control Officer is the only man who may give the command to fire. Knowing the target (a balloon) was almost out of range, I requested permission to fire.

The FCO said, "Negative. Stand by!" After a moment, he commanded, "Fire!"

Our bursts fell short of the target each time. It was certainly nothing like our firing the preceding April on the San Diego Range.

SPARRING AROUND

One Sunday afternoon amid calm seas and bright and sunny temperatures around 70 to 75 degrees, Johnny and I were working out on the top deck. A few others were around exercising and soaking up the beautiful weather. Johnny and I had finished our calisthenics, so we sparred around a little bit.

Capt. Richey was watching and remarked that he used to box at the Coast Guard Academy. In fact, I believe he said he was on the boxing team there.

Johnny said, "That's great! Would you like to spar around for a bit?"

The captain said, "Sure."

Johnny took off his mitts before I could get mine off and told me that I was going to box with the captain.

I said, "No, I'm not. This is your party."

Johnny wheedled, "Come on, Walt. You're just going to spar around."

I was leery of boxing the captain because I knew it was strictly against military regulations for an officer and an enlisted man to compete physically against each other in sports.

Capt. Richey (his rank was commander, but he was the captain of the ship) was 33 to 35 years old, about 5 feet, 11 in. tall, and 160 pounds. At that time I was maybe 6 feet, 165 pounds, and almost 23. We were probably about even because of his experience at the Academy, but he was 10 years older.

I didn't have much experience, but I was younger and faster, quicker on the reflexes. That told the story, as I beat my opponent to the punch most of the time and weaved out of the way of his punches. The captain was good. I enjoyed sparring with him, and he enjoyed the exercise.

Afterward, Johnny said he thought I had the best of the captain, but it was all in fun. If the captain had come out and exercised with us more often, I'm sure he could have taught us quite a bit.

SWIM CALL

During his watch on Feb. 2, 1952, RM2 Barnes received a radio dispatch stating,

```
Effective 12 Feb 1952 transfer
Walters Elmer D 275-577
PROREP OINC Cogard Radio Station
Westport, etc.
```

The District Office wanted to put me on the beach again after two years. Soon after hearing this, I took a copy directly down to the wardroom, where I found the XO. I showed him the message and stated that I wanted to remain on the *Strait,* and, with all due respect, I would appreciate whatever he could do when he filed his reports at the District Office in Seattle.

Days later, after we moored at Pier 70, my orders were changed. RM2 Barnes was delighted to take my place in Westport because he had a wife and two children.

Early in March, I was promoted to RM1. Shortly after, we went on weather patrol to Ocean Station UNCLE, now located where NAN formerly was. Because this was probably my last patrol, I really enjoyed the hot weather and the swim calls, which were usually on Saturday afternoons.

Swim calls were usually expected before they were announced, but no one was supposed to jump the gun and dive in ahead of time because the ship was supposed to come to a complete stop—dead in the water. A shark watch meant putting a small boat over the windward side and standing about 50 or 60 feet from the ship. In the small boat there would be two men with rifles (Garands were what we had then), and they would stand watch for sharks. The swimmers were allowed to swim only between the small boat and the ship. A cargo net was lowered over the side for the swimmers to climb aboard.

One Saturday, we had known there was to be a swim call, and many of us got ready. When the PA system announced "Swim call in 10 minutes!" many of us jumped the gun—and jumped in!

When I came to the surface, I saw nothing but the fantail (stern) ahead of me and drifting away. I'm no great swimmer—in fact, I'm very poor—but I swam for all I was worth. Most of the others were ahead of me, and I'll bet I had to swim 200 yards to get back to the ship. I climbed up the cargo net and lay out on deck the rest of the afternoon.

OFFICERS AND GENTLEMEN

A new officer, Ensign Knowles, had come aboard at the last in-port period. He was an ex-Air Corps B-17 pilot and decided to switch to the Coast Guard.

GQ was held at the usual time of 1300 (1 p.m.), and we had surface firing exercises. After we secured from GQ, I lay below in the watchstanders' quarters, where my bunk was located.

An announcement from the PA blurted out: "Walters RM1, lay to the bridge!"

I went up to the bridge, and there Ens. Knowles modestly asked, "Would you show me how you operate the computer for surface fire, if you're free?"

I said, "Yes, sir. I'd be glad to show you."

He followed me up to the Fire Control Station, where I removed the canvas cover, then the metal cover of the unit, and wound it up, explaining the procedure to Knowles step by step, using a hypothetical problem. He understood, he said, and with no questions, he left. I secured the unit and returned below deck.

I had barely reached my quarters when the order came: "Walters RM1, report to the wardroom immediately!"

I hurried to the ward room where Lt. Comdr. Brodie 4th, the XO—with Ens. Knowles hiding behind him—confronted me.

"Walters, just what the hell are you telling Mr. Knowles? He says you don't know the first thing about running that computer!"

"Sir?" I replied. "I explained everything I've been taught, and I've been operating it for two years. Mr. Knowles had no questions when I explained everything to him 10 minutes ago."

Brodie demanded, " I want you to take *me* up there and show *me* just what the hell you're doing!"

I led the way out of the wardroom with Brodie behind me and Knowles bringing up the rear. As I removed the canvas cover, then the metal cover, and started to wind the unit up for the third time that day, I reiterated, "A year ago in April, our ship got 11 out of 12 shots through the screen on the San Diego Gunnery Range." I was reminding Brodie of our excellent surface firing in which I played no small part, but he remained unresponsive.

I went through the entire procedure, including an imaginary target, its course and speed. When everything clicked off with the exact range, we were on target.

Brodie pondered for a minute, glanced at Knowles, who was standing meekly aside, then gruffly demanded of me, "Okay, button it up and secure!" He immediately scurried off, with Knowles trying to keep up behind.

As I secured the unit, I thought, those two officers must think they aren't the least bit obligated to apologize. I felt better when I considered the source.

X. TROUBLED OFFICERS

During that patrol, we had a call that some mysterious flares were seen about 100 to 200 miles south of our station. We had to cruise to that area and set up a standard search pattern with a grid, but we found nothing. A commercial airline pilot had reported it. After a day or so of searching, we returned to our assigned area.

This was in the days of UFO scares. We had all read stories of strange happenings, but none were ever proved.

Not more than a day later, we received another message that more flares had been sighted in that same area. The *Strait* cruised there again, and we set up the same search pattern but still found nothing.

On May 2, 1952, the *Bering Strait* returned from UNCLE. I had made my last patrol.

FIRE WATCH

When we arrived at Todd Shipyard, there was some deck welding that had to be done. This kind of work is often done after normal working hours, sometimes late in the evening.

One day my section was on duty, and the engineering officer came into our watchstanders' quarters. "Walters," he said, "you have a fire watch tonight. It's from 1800 to 2000 on the main deck, starboard side, forward."

"Fire watch?" I asked. "That's an assignment for nonrated men [seamen or firemen], sir."

The EO responded, "I said *you* have a fire watch!"

"But I'm the duty radioman," I answered, "which means I can't perform two assignments. Anyway, the 13th Coast Guard District regulations flatly state that no radioman is to stand any watch [aside from radio duties] in port other than quarter-deck watches in an emergency."

The EO shouted, "I don't give a damn about your 13th regulations! I said *you* have a fire watch, and *you* had better be there."

Knowing that I was upsetting him, I agreed. "Yes, sir! I'll stand that watch, *but* as soon as possible I will report this to Mr. Getz, the communications officer [my boss], as soon as he comes aboard from liberty."

Insisting on the last word, the EO said, "*You* just be there at 1800."

During evening chow, this person (an officer and a gentleman?) came by my table specifically to bother me while I was eating. "*You* be up there at 1800!" he barked.

After finishing my meal, I made sure I was at the appointed area on time, where I met the shipyard welder, who simply asked me to stand by. The watch went without incident except for putting out a few sparks from the welding. After my two-hour watch, I lay below.

After the morning meal and before the officers' breakfast, I rushed up to officers' country, where I located Mr. Getz in his stateroom. I reported the fire watch incident to him, and he became very agitated. He left immediately to report it to the XO.

At morning reports, before 0800, the entire ship's company was mustered on the fantail in its respective divisions. After reports, roll call, and assignments from the XO to the Division officers, the latter were dismissed to their divisions. The EO was then called "front and center" to face the XO and the CO.

The XO, Lt. Comdr. R. D. Brodie 4th, stated emphatically, loud and clear (in so many words), "The 13th Coast Guard District Rules and Regulations clearly state that 'Under no circumstances is any radioman to be assigned any watch in port, other than a quarter-deck watch in an emergency.' Furthermore, *no officer in this command* will ignore this directive!"

The XO then dismissed the EO to his division station.

Word got around eventually about what triggered that stern reprimand, and I became known as "the man who put an officer on report."

DISCHARGED

On June 9, 1952, I was called into the ship's office to sign or not to sign papers for my discharge. The XO escorted me into the captain's cabin, where Comdr. Richey swore me into the CG Reserves for three years before I signed my discharge papers. Federal law at that time stated that every able-bodied male of a certain age was obligated to the government for a total of eight years. I had served five years of active duty; therefore, if I wanted to be discharged, I had to agree to join the Reserves for the remaining three years.

I hung around for a week after my discharge and attended the ship's picnic at Beaver Lake, east of Lake Washington. Shortly after the picnic, I boarded the CMSTP&P (Milwaukee Railroad) for Chicago, and then the New York Central for Rochester.

XI. SETTLED DOWN

For a month after arriving back home, I did nothing but loaf. I bought a car, a 1950 Ford, and really enjoyed cruising around. Transition from a regimented military life to a civilian life takes time.

My brothers and other friends said, "Now you're a veteran and you served your time, so you have to settle down now and get married and raise a family and join the club like the rest of us."

I thought, is that all there is? I wasn't sure I wanted that. I think now I allowed too many other people to influence me.

I soon got out of the habit of being responsible. I drifted around between two or three local jobs, and I didn't really care whether I kept them. The GI Bill offered me a chance for a four-year college degree, and I even inquired into enrolling in the University of Washington, in Seattle. My plans were to go there or to a radio school, where I would get a commercial license for the Merchant Marine.

In August 1952 I met Arlene through my already-married friends. Three months later we were married. She was divorced with three children: Sherryl, Richard, and Bonny. For two years I worked at a lumberyard and delivered construction materials in the wintertime. In the summer I worked as a roofer.

Our daughter, Deborah Ann, was born on Aug. 15, 1953. Just before she was to start school, we learned that she was, as the specialists declared, "mildly retarded." She now resides in an adult care home in New York state and is able to do menial work in a supervised group. She seems happy to be living with her peers.

1955: WHAM-TV

I attended a radio and electronics school in 1954 on the GI bill.

In 1955, I earned my 1st Class Radiotelephone and 2nd Class Radiotelegraph licenses. Shortly after that, I was hired by WHAM-AM-FM-TV Studios in Rochester. It was before videotape and even before comedian Foster Brooks worked there. It was very enjoyable work, but I was not using my engineering skills to the fullest extent. I was working in the studios as a cameraman and doing film shading, audio control, and minor maintenance.

Television was only 8 or 10 years old in Rochester broadcasting. Most of the programming didn't start until noon. When I came on board, WHAM-TV was broadcasting in the mornings at 7:45 and signing off at midnight or 1 a.m. with the National Anthem and a picture of the American flag. Two other channels shared the same station and transmitting equipment, taking turns broadcasting for years. All three channels shared the same antenna tower on Pinnacle Hill in Rochester.

During that time, most of the programs were broadcast live, produced right in the studios, because videotape hadn't been invented yet. The *Home Cooking Show* was telecast in the morning with Trudy McNall and emceed by Ross Weller. Trudy was a Cornell graduate, a wonderful cook, and very gifted at talking and working in her studio kitchen at the same time. Ross kept busy with his gift of gab, assisting Trudy.

My first program as a cameraman was, I think, called *Stop the Clock*. Ted Jackson, the emcee, would call people on the telephone and ask them a question, giving them 15 seconds to answer correctly to win a prize. My job was to hold the camera steady on a large 12-in. wall clock for 15 seconds so that everyone in the TV audience could see whether the contestant could answer the question in time.

The camera was mounted on wooden legs (tripods) in those days.

During the afternoons, I "rode gain on the audio," which meant I worked in the studio control room with the producer and the film shade man. I controlled the audio gain throughout the programs.

Usually at 1 p.m., the afternoon movie would be shown, allowing for breaks. That was a very relaxed part of the day. One of the main sponsors for this Monday-Friday program was a milk cooperative. We actually had to have one quart of milk delivered every day so the announcer could hold up the milk to talk about it. A refrigerator was wheeled into the studio and the door held open showing about 8 or 10 empty cartons inside, but only that one "live" quart was held up for display.

One day I had not planted the refrigerator too evenly on the dolly before I wheeled it into the studio. As Ann, the announcer, jerked open the door, the fridge started to reel around on its dolly, and the empty milk cartons tipped at different angles. The producer went into shock until the cartons settled down. Ann went right on talking, not noticing anything wrong.

The bosses made it clear to me that that was not to happen again.

Arlene and I had another daughter, Dorothy Arlene, born Aug. 19, 1955, while I was working at WHAM.

1955-58: GENERAL DYNAMICS

Television was in a state of transition. Videotape came out, which meant that more and more programs were being broadcast that did not have to be produced live. That meant cutting back on personnel, especially producers and video and audio men in the studios. I was able to move over to Stromberg-Carlson Co., which owned WHAM. In 1956, General Dynamics bought Stromberg-Carlson and formed the electronics division (GD/E). I worked there in engineering in the Research & Advanced Development Laboratory for five years.

EUCLID (Electronic Utilization of Components for the Logical Interpretation of Data), developed at Stromberg, was in its infancy. It involved using discreet components, like transistors, diodes, resistors, etc., on printed wiring boards.

On Sept. 25, 1958, Arlene gave birth to our son, Daniel Elmer Walters. I have always been very proud of all three of our children as they grew into adulthood and as they are today.

XII. 'IF ANYTHING CAN GO WRONG, IT WILL.'*

One of the projects I was involved in at work was the Rock Island Railroad Car Sorter System, which used electromechanical multigang telephone relays and solid-state electronic circuitry in its design.

The largest project I was assigned to was the AN/GLR-1, Passive Reconnaissance System, the "Big Ear." This project involved the gathering, interpretation, and deciphering of both Comint and Elant (communications and electronics) signals. Stations were to be installed in West Germany, Turkey, and later, under another contractor, in Japan, to listen in on the USSR.

At first I worked on the design of a "signal analyzer," interpreting various electronic signals such as Pulse Width, Pulse Repetition Period, and Scan Period, which were to be isolated from noise greater than the signal itself. That was a challenge to many engineers. A year later, when I looked at the schematics, I hardly recognized how the engineers had redesigned the system since I first worked on it.

The engineer I worked with was Bill Tyrlick, a graduate of Purdue University and a brilliant young man who, I'm sure, went on to bigger things.

FIELD SERVICE

In 1961 I switched to the Field Service Department and was sent to Keesler Air Force Base in Biloxi, Miss. to help install and maintain the system where the Air Force personnel would train on it.

In July I went back up north and brought Arlene, Deb, Dot, and Dan back to Biloxi, where we rented a beautiful home on West Beach Boulevard right across from the Mississippi Sound.

---

*Murphy's Law.

The first day our family was there, Danny was playing with his new jet airplane that I had bought when I flew up to Rochester to pick up the family, and— "ker-splash!"—he fell backward right into the middle of our fish pond, with 10 bright orange goldfish trying to evade him.

Our family thoroughly enjoyed the hot and sunny weather in Biloxi. We were there for six months, and when the contract expired, we returned to Rochester. Sometime later I started a new project.

NEW PROJECTS

The new project was labeled AUTODIN—Automatic Digital Network. It was a Defense Communications Worldwide High-Speed Common User Data Communications System. It provided both direct user-to-user and store-and-forward message switching service for the Department of Defense. The DSTE (Digital Subscriber Terminal Equipment) consisted of a Common Control Unit, Universal Keyboard, Card Reader, Low-Speed Card Punch, High-Speed Card Punch, High-Speed Paper Tape Punch, Low-Speed Paper Tape Punch, and a Page Printer.

My responsibility was initially to test these devices with other engineers. After three or four months, I was assigned to head up the overall testing of the entire system, employing 12 to 15 men, working on a 3-shift operation, 7 days a week.

This project was completed and phased out around 1969.

AUTEC (Atlantic Underwater Test and Evaluation Center) was a Navy sonar buoy test program. It was very interesting. Two other engineers and I made daily trips through the winter from GD/E Division in Rochester to the middle of Seneca Lake on a large barge. Bob Jackson, John Leahy, and I did the testing. We would drive our car to the waterfront, park it, and take our test equipment and lunches out on the pier. An old cabin cruiser would be waiting for us, and we would have to jump from the pier down on top of the cruiser roof. Then we would chug out through the dense vapor, with the cruiser skipper commanding, of course, to the barge anchored on the lake.

This project was still being investigated and under contract with the Navy when General Dynamics decided to scrap it, along with closing the Electronics Division in Rochester.

One of the best men I ever had the privilege to work under was Len Kure, a Case University graduate from Cleveland. We worked together from 1960, the Biloxi days, to late 1970. We always got along fine, and he seemed to have more faith in my capabilities than some of the other managers.

ROCHESTER PRODUCTS DIVISION OF GMC

As GD/E closed in 1971, many of us went our different ways. I was hired by Rochester Products, a division of General Motors, and Len was picked up by Railway Signal in Rochester. A few years later, I heard that he had succumbed to leukemia.

Arlene decided that she would like to take in foster children; she had become unable to do bookkeeping because of her crippling arthritis. Through the Catholic Family Center of the Rochester Diocese, we took in maybe 40 to 50 infants, from the time they left the hospital until they were adopted, over a span of 8 or 9 years.

In 1966 the Center was having a hard time placing an infant girl, Diane, who had been born with Down syndrome. One day they asked us to consider caring for the child. After discussing it with our family, friends, and physicians (who did not recommend it), we decided for that very same reason that Diane needed us. She required constant care and digitalis every day; two or three times during her first two years, we had to rush her to the hospital because she was turning blue, drowning in her own lung fluids.

Diane was with us until Arlene's death and remained in another foster home until her own death in 1984 at age 18.

Arlene's arthritis had continued to worsen. Pain-killing drugs increasingly weakened her. In 1971 she developed pneumonia and became progressively worse, spending six months in the hospital at one point and one month in and the next out many times until she could not fight any longer. She died in January 1973.

THE BAERS, 1965

Two very good friends of Arlene's and mine were Jack and Dot Baer. Arlene and Dot first met because they were in the local parish church ladies' group. We all began visiting back and forth and playing cards with other couples, too. Jack was a retired World War II Navy chief petty officer and had worked at Eastman Kodak for 20 years.

One clear, crisp Saturday in the fall of 1965, Jack and Dot had a little spat during breakfast. After Jack finished, he went outside to cut the grass with his riding mower.

Sometime later there was a loud bang, and all the windows in their house shook. Dot scurried outside just in time to see Jack turn around the corner of the house. She went tearing after him, shaking her fist at him and yelling for all she was worth. Jack didn't know what her problem was; he couldn't hear a word she was saying, so he kept right on mowing.

Later Dot called Arlene about the four of us getting together for cards that night. She told Arlene about the spat she had had with Jack. "He was so rude that he deliberately ran his riding mower into the side of the house and made such a loud bang that all the windows shook!"

"When did this happen, Dot?" Arlene asked.

"Well, it had to be—around 10:30."

"Dot, that wasn't Jack making all that noise," said Arlene. "That was a jet plane overhead, breaking the sound barrier!"

The line was quiet for a few seconds, then Dot said, "It was? Well, I'm still not going to apologize to him!"

Later that evening at the Baers's, we talked about the jet breaking the sound barrier and making all that noise. Jack hadn't heard it because he'd been driving the mower. When we told him what Dot had blamed him for, he simply smiled and shrugged. "That makes me feel pretty good, knowing I've been blamed by all the village wives for shaking their windows."

MY FIRST AMATEUR RADIO RIG

It was around that time, in the 1960s, that I was accepted as a Life Member into the Society of Wireless Pioneers. The charter reads: "Dedicated—to the men who went down to the sea in ships as Wireless Telegraphers and all those who have earned their living 'pounding brass' as wireless radio ops since the days of Marconi."

I have also been a radio amateur since early 1954; my license, or call, is K2JT1. The first rig (transmitter) I built was one from *The Radio Amateur's Handbook,* also known as the radio amateur's "bible." It was for 75-watts on voice and 100-watts on Morse Code. It was a compact unit that was switchable to five different amateur bands, known as 160, 80, 40, 20, and 10/11 meters (3.5 to 28 Mc. or Mhz.). No transistors were available in those days because it was all vacuum tube theory. I used a 6AG7 for a modified Pierce oscillator. The next three stages were using 6V6s, and the final stage was a pair of 807s connected in parallel. This nice little transmitter was featured in *The Radio Amateur's Handbook* from 1948 through the mid '50s.

Building my own set was very interesting and challenging. Refining and tuning it was to me the very essence of amateur radio, but I soon tired of having an avocation, similar to a vocation in electronics design, which I was doing 40 hours a week.

I have known amateurs who worked all day in electronics repair or design and rushed home to "fire up" their amateur rigs to talk into the wee morning hours to another radio amateur, night after night.

CGC UNIMAK

Having remained in the Coast Guard Reserve, I attended weekend meetings and served two weeks' active duty every year for 31 years.

One of the two-week cruises I requested was on the *CGC Unimak,* a WAVP like the *Bering Strait.* The *Unimak* was scheduled for a trip from Yorktown, Va. to Yarmouth, Nova Scotia and back in October 1972. I reported aboard on a Sunday afternoon after visiting my brother and his family in Williamsburg, Va., where they lived at that time.

Shortly after I was shown to my berth on the ship, all the lights went out and everything fell quiet. After a couple of minutes I heard the voices of people scurrying through the passageway. The emergency lighting came on, and I asked what was happening.

One of the voices said, "We're looking for the electrical panel. Maybe you can help us."

I said, "Sure, I'll be glad to if I can."

I was still wearing my dress khakis after reporting aboard. I followed the other two men; one turned out to be the EO, a young fellow with a heavy beard. All three of us rushed down a couple of ladders (flights of stairs) to a panel, and as I held a flashlight, the other two found the right circuit breakers and got the generators on. Before leaving port, the crew had evidently cut off shore power and were switching to ship's power when the problem occurred. I was glad I could help, even if it was only in a small way.

Shortly after, I reported to the XO, a lieutenant commander on the port wing, who was "singling up the lines" before casting off. At that moment, there was a "frump-frump" noise, and looking up, I saw two dark clouds coming from the stack. As they slowly wafted over our heads, it started to rain—oil droplets.

Luckily, on my way up from the engine room, I had taken off my blouse and dropped it in my stateroom, which was the old aviation officers' room, just forward of the general mess deck. I had on my long-sleeved dress shirt, of course, and black oil spots began to show up all over my shirt and trousers. The XO looked at me pitifully because he knew he was in the same shape.

Eventually we managed to leave the pier with no further incidents. But our second night out, the alarms went off, waking me from a sound sleep. "Fire! Fire!" someone was yelling.

I had my trousers and shoes on and was out the door, but not as fast as my roommate, who had been sleeping on the other side of the room. He went right past me and out the door, but his pants fell down as he bounded up the ladder because he hadn't zipped his fly.

My GQ station was on the bridge in Radar, where I reported. The fire was down in the engine room; some packing had overheated and ignited.

A day later, the freshwater evaporators gave out. At noon meal in the wardroom, the XO announced a ration of "one gallon of water per day per man." As it turned out, we diverted our course to go into New London Submarine Base to get the "evaps" repaired.

We arrived at the base at about 2000 and promptly cruised right up to the pier—in fact, right into the pier. We stove a hole 4 feet by 5 feet into our port bow. Pilings sometimes don't give too much. Now, besides getting our evaps fixed, we also had to have our crew work half the night repairing the hull.

All repairs effected, we were going to leave around 0200 or so. The Navy offered tug assistance to help us out. The Coast Guard use a Navy

CGC Unimak: The ship that seemed to operate under Murphy's Law. Built in 1942, she is 311 feet long, with a beam of 41 feet. She is twin-screwed, displacing 2,800 tons and drawing 13 feet. Her primary mission was the underway training of reserves.

tug? Never! So we departed the pier and promptly lost power and steering.

We began to drift across the river toward some nuclear submarines tied there, so the Navy offered to guide us until we got powered up again. Soon we had power and steering again. We were all set, so we waved off the Navy tug.

Five minutes later we lost power and steering again and were drifting around in circles, closer to the subs. The Navy tug returned in a half hour and guided us along until we got power once again. The Bridge hailed the tug and said, "Thanks; we're all set now," but they ignored us. They escorted us all the way to the mouth of the Thames and almost to the open sea.

Suddenly one morning as we passed through a lobster fishing area, the engines came to a full stop, and we were drifting. I went outside and saw five or six officers and some of the crew milling around the fantail.

"What are we doing?" I asked.

In a low voice, someone replied out of the side of his mouth, "We fouled a screw. One of the lobster lines got tangled in it."

The Coast Guard frowns on that—at least, the *real* Coast Guard does.

We did fine for the next few days, except every so often we could hear the now familiar "fromp—fromp," and if we were outside, we rushed inside before the oily rain hit.

As we arrived in Nova Scotia, the harbor pilot came aboard. It was a beautiful day in late fall. The pilot was saying, "This is a typical day here in Yarmouth—clear and crisp, nice fresh air. No pollution here."

Just then— "fromp—fromp." Oil rained down on some of the fishing boats as we passed, and we were trailing a small oil slick up the channel.

Returning to Yorktown, we encountered nothing of incidence. Some of the men practically begged me to write a report on the conditions throughout the ship, but I still had time to serve before I got my retirement papers, and I didn't dare blow the whistle until later.

I had never been in a wardroom where there was such open talk and criticism about the CO. The XO was in the middle of it, too.

As we approached Chesapeake Bay, a merchant ship overtook us, heading south. The captain decided to relieve the Officers of the Day (OOD) and gave the command to make a standard turn to the left to allow the merchant ship to pass. We continued to turn left for 10 or 12 circles—once again, because the steering was lost.

Finally, the freighter was long gone and we made our turn into the bay to within two or three miles from Yorktown pier. Then orders were given to have two Coast Guard 44-footers come out and pull us *broadside* all the way to the pier. This brave maneuver had to take at least two or three hours or more.

When I was released from duty, I went to the captain's cabin, where the XO also was, and requested permission to leave the ship. I felt compelled to add, "Captain, this is the only ship I was ever on where all your drills are the real thing!"

The captain and the XO smiled faintly.

A SUGGESTION PAYS OFF

In 1973, when I was working at Rochester Products (GM), I was asked by supervision to change my classification from Electrician to Communications/Electrician.

An electrician apprentice was working in that spot at the time. He quit and walked off the job one day after a fiery argument with his supervisor. He was a very nervous type of fellow and had a hard time working under pressure. I had been asked to work overtime, at different times, to assist him in repairing radios or PA system amplifiers. He had no set plan of attack on any single problem, to say nothing of having to repair two or three systems that broke down all at once. Gradually, many time clocks had broken down, the fire alarm system had not worked throughout the plant for months, and many audio amplifiers needed repair on the PA system.

Consequently, when he quit, the department head of Building Utilities did not encourage him to think it over. The supervisors checked résumés in the Personnel Department and found that my background (training and experience at General Dynamics) seemed more suitable than that of anyone else.

One of the requirements of a Communications/Electrician rating was a Second Class Radiotelephone license for the repair of two-way radios. Bob, the man who quit, had tried and failed numerous times to obtain his FCC license. I had had my First Class Radiotelephone and Second Class Radiotelegraph licenses for almost 20 years by then, with years of experience in radio.

Part of my assignment was the maintenance and repair of the time system, master clock, and 40 to 50 time recorder clocks scattered throughout the plant. Later in the mid-1970s a satellite plant was built about 2 or 3 miles away. That plant had its own clock system, separate fire alarm and proprietary system, and its own PA system. That was my responsibility too, and I would have to take a company bus (van) every so often to do repairs there.

That meant keeping up on all repairs and not allowing the work to pile up. I had to be able to work on my own, and I was able to come and go as I pleased.

The fire alarm system, for example, was an electromechanical type of system that required constant cleaning of all the units throughout the factory. The electrical contacts within the units would get dirty because of the oily, misty atmosphere.

Because the system was so old, it took maybe six or more hours to troubleshoot in trying to locate one specific transmitter (unit) to repair it, and in the meantime the entire fire alarm system was out of service. In the late 1970s I came up with the idea of installing two small low-voltage bulbs in each loop box located equal distances from one another around the outer perimeter of the plant. By traveling around the plant and simply observing the two little lights and the way they flashed, I could pinpoint the location of the transmitter in 15 minutes or less. That reduced troubleshooting time from 6 hours to 15 minutes, but mainly the fire alarm system was not out of service for very long at a time.

Jim Sullivan, a brilliant young electrician (a graduate of the University of Arizona) was assigned to work with me. I offered to share my idea with him if he would assist in installing the system lights.

That idea won us a company award of $15,000, which Sullivan and I split. GM had and still has, I presume, an excellent suggestion program, and good suggestions are well rewarded. I made a few suggestions over the years, but that was the last and the most profitable.

The time system required about 40 to 50 percent of my time, repairing the Simplex clocks, which operated mostly on cams and springs. Newer clocks were designed to operate on solenoids. They were all electromechanical, like the fire alarm system.

A few months before I retired in 1991, the company was investigating and eventually installed a new electronic fire alarm system.

BEST FRIENDS

One of the best friends I ever had was Lefty LaDue, who lived near Hilton. Although he was two years younger than I, we had known each other practically all our lives. When we had both been discharged, myself in 1952 and Lefty from the Air Force in 1955, we became close friends.

Both of us were active in the local American Legion post, and I followed Lefty through the chairs as we both became past commanders. I was Lefty's campaign manager when he was elected to a county vice commander post, and the next year he was my campaign manager when I was elected county adjutant, then county vice commander the year after that.

We were both active in boys' baseball programs every summer for years. I had coached and managed Little League and Pony League teams, and then we teamed up for the 15-to-17-year-olds' team. Lefty managed and I assisted, with two other men coaching. Lefty had a second nickname— "Hook" LaDue—pinned on him because he had had quite a curve ball in his playing days. He was only 5 feet, 5 in. tall, or he might have had a professional career.

In 1959 or '60, I persuaded Lefty to join the Coast Guard Reserves. From a flight engineer in a SAC bomber to a diesel mechanic on small boats and larger ships was no big jump for Lefty. He was very proficient in both skills. He had a great rapport with his men, not only in the Reserves but also at work and on the ballfield.

In later years, Lefty went on active duty in the Coast Guard. In 1984, he suffered a massive heart attack. He was the most congenial and down-to-earth fellow I've ever met. I miss him to this day and always will.

MEETING JOE DiMAGGIO

About May or June 1974, I received orders to report to the Coast Guard Instructor Training (IT) School at Alameda, California. Given a training voucher, I made arrangements to fly UAL from Rochester to Chicago, then from Chicago to San Francisco via DC-10.

The Alameda Coast Guard Base is small and compact. You can walk anywhere on the base, but I rented a compact auto for golfing and sightseeing in the San Francisco area. I played golf frequently over the two-week period with Lt. Tom Brie from New York and a young Lt. Carolyn Alexander from California. Her husband, David, was an engineer with a lettuce company in Salinas. They breed and train dogs now, and Carolyn, I believe, is retired from the military.

On the first Friday, we had an exam covering the first week's work; then we were dismissed for the weekend.

Leaving the base, I drove into the Fisherman's Wharf area to enjoy the scenery and the atmosphere. I had been there quite a bit before, and I liked the area.

The DiMaggio Family Restaurant was located upstairs over the Ripley "Believe It or Not" Building. Upon entering by the outside staircase, I saw the cocktail lounge on the right and the restaurant to the left.

After visiting the bar for a cocktail and a chat with the bartender, I arose to leave, when I instantly recognized the great former New York Yankee baseball star, Joe DiMaggio himself, sitting in a booth with some of his old cronies.

Walking by, I paused and said, "Mr. DiMaggio, hello!"

I was dumbfounded as he arose, stepped forward, and extended his hand, which was twice the size of mine.

"Yes, hello," he said. "How are you?"

"I would be remiss in my duties to my friends back home if I didn't say hello when I saw you," I told him.

He laughed and asked my name and where I was from.

"Rochester, New York," I told him.

The great Yankee Clipper remarked rather fondly, "Oh, yes, the Rochester Red Wings!"

He invited me to sit down and join him in the booth as he ignored his three friends, all in their 70s, I would guess. They remained seated, drinking coffee and talking among themselves.

I couldn't believe it! Here I was, taking up this man's time, and he was asking me about things back in New York and what I was doing in the Coast Guard in California. I was actually sitting next to my boyhood idol, and he was asking me all about myself!

We sat and chatted for about ten minutes, and finally I arose and said, "Mr. DiMaggio, I have taken up enough of your time. I should be leaving."

He stood up and extended his hand again, saying, "Elmer, it was a pleasure. Be sure you stop in again."

The man exuded class. I had always heard how great a gentleman he was, and now I had seen it first-hand.

The next day I picked up the *San Francisco Chronicle* and read in the second section that Joe DiMaggio had lost a court case two days earlier. He had sued a neighbor who built a fence that blocked Joe's view of the San Francisco Bay from his home.

Joe DiMaggio died in March 1999, shortly before the publication of this book. Baseball lost one of its greatest stars.

XIII. FLYING

In the late '70s, when people asked me what I did in my spare time, I told them, "I soar in a sailplane (or glider)."

Frequently their answer would be, "Wow! I've always wanted to try that myself, but I never got around to doing it."

At age 50, I finally got around to doing it because I knew soaring would be the challenge I was seeking. My lessons were in a Schweitzer SGS 2-33A when I first started in Vacaville, Calif. and later in Hamlin, N.Y. Some flight hours later I progressed to an IS-28B *Lark*, a fairly high-performance machine. The *Lark's* wing span is 57 feet, as opposed to the SGS 2-33A, which I believe has a wing span of only 37 feet.

The sailplane is very impressive with its narrow, slim fuselage and its high T-tail. After the preflight checkout, a nylon towline is connected to the hook in the front of the sailplane and its other end is hooked to the towplane waiting 200 feet ahead.

When ready, the sailplane pilot wags his rudder as a signal, and the towplane pilot does the same. The sailplane pilot then gives the wing runner a "thumbs up," signifying that he is ready for his wing to be lifted off the ground and held horizontally.

Keeping the sailplane straight behind the towplane is not always easy, especially with any kind of crosswind. After being towed 200-250 feet, the sailcraft will lift off gently and the pilot must keep it low and directly behind the towplane. As the towplane lifts off and starts climbing, the sailplane assumes its position just a little above it.

The towplane pilot will almost always know where the "lift" is and get the sailplane to the desired altitude, where the sailplane will release and be free of the "umbilical" cord. This is the point in flight where the sailplane pilot experiences the freedom and silence of soaring.

The sailplane soars across the sky from thermal to thermal (rising bodies of warm air) and climbs from 2,000 to 3,000 feet in minutes. The thermals could be coming off some freshly plowed fields in the late spring, a paved blacktop parking lot in the winter, the open area of the desert floor, or a mountainous ridge. The pilot practices stalls, wingovers, and slow flight back to the airport. All these maneuvers are extremely exhilarating, and spinning in a sailplane is thrilling, to say the least.

Then comes the moment when the pilot approaches pattern entry altitude and makes a decision to terminate the flight. There is no room for mistakes as he goes through his checklist for landing.

No traffic on the runway, none approaching on "final," and none approaching in an opposite pattern, so it is clear that he has a "go" for landing.

When he comes to a stop and unbuckles his harness, he thinks, *That was great! What a nice flight! I can't wait to get back up there again—"where you truly soar with the eagles."*

Although soaring was one of my greatest thrills, I had decided to go to aviation ground school to learn more about airports, cross-country flights, and maybe more about weather. The ground school was absorbing, and I became more fascinated with flight. Just before finishing ground school, I started to take flight lessons in a Piper PA28-140 but mostly in a Cessna C-152.

1981: 1S-28B Lark (high performance) sailplane.

POWER FLIGHT

My first six or eight 1-hour lessons in power flight were taught by a young college student trying to earn money for school and to build up flight time for the airlines. He found he had overloaded his schedule of instructions and his schoolwork, so he had to cut back on students.

A fellow ground school classmate told me more than once that I should contact Gerry, his instructor.

Gerry and I hit it off right away, because he was a radio amateur, as I had been since the early '50s. Of course, I had already had my 1st Class Radiotelephone and 2nd Class Radiotelegraph licenses since 1954.

Gerry was a few years younger than I, and he had been flying for years. He prided himself on never having had a student fail a flight exam given by an examiner. When Gerry said you were ready to solo, you were ready to solo, and when he said you were ready for your flight test, you were ready. Most flight instructors seem to know when a student is ready for the next step.

One of the most memorable sessions I had with Gerry was when I started to taxi on the ramp toward the run-up area in a Cessna 152. I had a tendency to try to steer the plane with the wheel, along with the foot pedals for the rudder. Gerry had told me a few times before to simply steer with the foot controls on the ground.

On one particular day, I had forgotten and had my hands on the wheel trying to steer, when Gerry suddenly slapped my right arm off the wheel.

"Godammit, Elmer, you touch that wheel again and I'll break your arm!"

He didn't mean it, obviously, but he got his point across. That was all it took, because he got my attention, and I *never* forgot that lesson.

I soon learned to have complete faith in Gerry's flying abilities and his instructions. When he told me to "clear the area" (make sure there is no other airplane or anything in your practice area), then do an "accelerated stall," I would do it without hesitation. That is the point in flight instruction where most students drop out, if they're going to drop out. It's a little scary when you set a steep angle of altitude, continue increasing the power, and at the same time pull back on the yoke as far as it will go. The plane begins to stall; as you keep your wings level, the nose drops and you immediately recover and level off.

A year or two later, after I had taken some aerobatic instruction in a Citabria (Airbatic, spelled backward), I asked Gerry for a check ride in the Cessna 152 and some hood work. Then I enjoyed showing him a few spins he hadn't done in a long time.

It must have been late August or early September when I was ready for my second cross-country solo flight. Gerry signed the back of my book to make it official. He wanted me to fly from Brockport to Ithaca, at the foot of Cayuga Lake, then to Oswego County (Fulton), and finally back to Brockport.

Every day I checked the weather, and it seemed that every day it was either cloudy and overcast or raining. Day after day I waited, for one week, two weeks, then three weeks as the weather pattern continued. One day it looked halfway decent, with only a few scattered clouds. I called the Buffalo Aviation Weather and was told that there were scattered clouds at 3,500 feet and solid cover at Ithaca with an 800-foot base, but they should clear in a couple of hours.

Leaving home, I arrived at the Brockport Airport by 8 a.m., preflighted the airplane, fueled up, and called Buffalo Weather again at 9 a.m. The report was basically the same as before, so I waited anxiously for another hour.

At 10 a.m., I called again. The person on the phone said that most of the area of the central and western secion was fairly clear, with some broken clouds, and that solid cloud cover over the southern part of the Finger Lakes region was about an 800-foot ceiling but should be breaking up by 11 a.m.; I should have no trouble by the time I got there.

I said, "Fine. I'm opening up my flight plan. This is Cessna 152, 5 8 7 XRAY, color red and white, one person, departing 1100, en route direct to Ithaca, then to Oswego County, and return to Brockport; flying time, three hours."

1981-83: Cessna C -152, an excellent two-place trainer.

Climbing out over Brockport, I set the course for southeast to Ithaca and immediately called Rochester Tower as I entered its air space. They had me "squawk" (a certain code on the transponder so they could recognize my aircraft) and told me there was a "heavy" (large plane) coming up at 2000 off Runway 24. I immediately spotted him about two miles ahead and below. He would be long gone by the time I got there.

There certainly was more cloud cover than reported by Buffalo; Rochester was pretty well covered, and I saw only a hole in the clouds over the airport. The clouds were 1,000 feet below me as I cruised at 3,500.

I started thinking, *maybe I'm not supposed to be doing this.* VFR—Visual Flight Rules—require complete vision of the entire ground area. But I was determined to get on with my cross-country work and get it over with. Sometimes we do foolish things that we should be more cautious about. But I was confident, never more so in my ability than on that day.

Glancing down to my right through an opening in the clouds, I recognized the city of Canandaigua. As I got within 30 miles of Ithaca, I called Ithaca and asked about its weather. Still only a 900-foot ceiling and solid overcast.

I reported that I was diverting to Oswego County. Arriving at the Ithaca (VOR), I changed course to a north-northeast direction for Fulton (Oswego County).

About a half-hour from Fulton, I could see that it was quite clear along Lake Ontario, much clearer than it was to the south. Just dead ahead was a fairly large cloud; rising to 4,000 feet, I decided to go through it. Holding my altitude and horizontal level, I passed through the cloud after maybe 30 seconds. As I came out, the weather was clear as a bell, and directly ahead lay my destination.

Approaching Fulton, I called, "Oswego County Traffic, this is Cessna 5 8 7 XRAY, five miles out at 3,000, inbound from the south."

I observed some smoke blowing in a general easterly direction, so I entered the airport pattern for a northwesterly downwind.

After landing and taxiing to the ramp, I checked in at the little office and had the fellow there sign my logbook. The man refueled my airplane as I had a cup of 4-hour-old coffee. Shortly afterward, I departed Fulton to the west along the Lake Ontario shoreline, past Sodus Point, past Rochester to Hilton, then southwest to Brockport airport.

When I had the airport in sight, I called Buffalo Radio to close out my flight plan, then descended to pattern altitude, and landed. I was quite euphoric over the whole day's work, but when I checked with my flying instructor, he brought me back down to earth in a short time.

"You didn't do what you were supposed to do, Elmer," Gerry told me. "You didn't land at three different points, which is a *must*. You'll have to do it all over again."

After all that, I didn't think I should bother him with my flying on instruments. He would surely have gotten more gray hairs than he already had.

Later that evening I told my son Dan about my cross-country flight. He simply smiled, shook his head, and said, "I don't believe it. Better you than me!"

Dan was about ready to do his cross-countrys any day. I had complete faith in him and was sure that he would be more sensible than I.

Some airmen prefer flying planes with the steering wheels on the yokes, and some prefer a control stick between their legs. Most nowadays use a wheel on a yoke, and they control banking with the left hand and the throttle with the right hand, or vice-versa if they happen to be flying in the right-hand seat. Using a control stick in the center allows you to control it with the right hand while the left hand controls the throttle, prop pitch, and air brakes on a glider.

Maybe that's why I always preferred flying airplanes or seaplanes with control sticks, like the Citabria, the PT-17 Stearman, the Pitts S2S, or my own Starduster II. That type seems much more maneuverable and faster-responding.

Flying Earl Luce's "Cubby," a replica of a Piper Cub with 65 hp, was a joy. You would get the sense of just floating over the green pastures, cornfields, orchards, or woods. In the late fall, we would spot deer grazing 150 feet down below in a secluded pasture, and some might be ambling through the woods, completely innocent of any hunter who might be only 100 feet on the other side of the underbrush. Earl and I completely marveled at all that was going on down below.

One day Earl and I flew his Cubby down south of Batavia, where I was keeping my Starduster for a short time. The first time I flew there with Earl, I asked him where the farmer's airstrip was, so I could drive there and find exactly where it was in reference to a road map.

"I hate to tell you, Elmer," Earl said, "I've only flown here, so I have no idea where it is on the ground."

"That's great!" I replied sarcastically. "If I fly my plane here, how do I tell someone to pick me up there?"

"All I can say is, fly southwesterly until you spot the city of Batavia. Just three miles before Batavia, fly south-southwest for 5 minutes until you spot a green-and-white-striped silo top. Just south of that, you'll see a 2,000-foot east-west strip east of the woods with corn or beans on either side. You can't miss it, Elmer," he said.

Do you know what? He was right! If I followed his directions—and I did, quite often, later—I would come out with a heading right on that green and white silo top, exactly. It was another story if I flew in from any other direction.

Driving down to that farm strip, I turned south before the city of Batavia and went up and down those country roads for an hour or more, looking for a green-and-white-striped silo top. It was no easy task with the tall maple and oak trees lining the country roads until I found that silo. Then it was almost impossible to see the strip near the road. Earl's son, Matt, had found the road and strip for him the only time he drove down there.

Earl and I flew down to the strip one nice, warm day in August, just to pass the time and to see what was going on for a few minutes. We came in just over the tall oaks in front of the road, cut the power, and dipped the left wing as we slipped in just past the sheds and onto the grass strip, heading west. Coming to a stop, Earl spun the plane around and we taxied back to the parking area.

A couple of cars were parked near the old barn door entrance. As we went in the first room, there was an old Glenn Curtiss, high-wing, open-cockpit, pusher-type plane just sitting there gathering dust, dirt, and simply rotting away.

Earl told me a little about the history of the craft as we ambled into the inner room. Harold, the owner, and two other fellow pilots were sitting around the pot-bellied stove, just "shooting the bull."

"Pull up a chair," Harold said as I looked around.

The only chair I saw was an old overstuffed one that had seen better days 30 years earlier. Harold's dog, Fetch, was sprawled across it, and he looked as if he owned it, so I was not about to displace him.

Fred and Carl, the other two visitors, were restoring an old Piper Cub. In the darkness of the big room, I could see the frame of the fuselage resting on some blocks. The wing was lying off to the side, and the prop was stashed in the corner.

"Have some coffee," one of the guys suggested, as they offered us a couple of Styrofoam cups on the workbench, and the other poured.

Leaning against the bench, we sipped the coffee as Harold asked Earl about his "tailwind project," which he was building. I was more interested in all the old aircraft calendars hanging on the wall and all the old aircraft parts on the bench and the floor.

Finishing our coffee, we said our "s'longs" because we had to get back to Brockport. Going out the same way we had come in, my eyes were fixed on that old Curtiss "pusher." Earl almost had to drag me out of there and back to his aircraft.

I hopped in the front cockpit and held the foot brakes so Earl could hand-prop the plane, because that was the only way he could start it. But not this time. We tried everything to start that plane, but it would not so much as cough.

After a couple of minutes, Earl said, "Stay right there. I'll be back."

I remained right where I was, wondering what he was going to get—maybe a wrench or some fuel or a piece of wire; maybe there was a bad connection.

Soon he showed up with a bucket of water from the well near the back of the farmhouse. He removed the cowling and poured the entire bucket of water over the engine.

"What are you doing?" I said. "Are you crazy?"

He laughed. "Stand by, she'll start in a minute."

Replacing the cowling, he told me to hold the brakes again. As he pulled the prop part way through—*presto!*— the Cubby jumped to life and was running as smoothly as it ever had.

That day I learned there was more to flying than flight manuals and ground schools. A little bit of "using your head" and "ingenuity" goes a long way, but I wouldn't always recommend Earl's method.

When I started soaring, my instructor reprimanded me for being too light on the rudders. "That's one thing you'll have to change if you're ever going to soar," Debbie told me. She was an excellent instructor and multiengine-rated.

Much later, my power flight instructor, Jerry Barlow, told me I was good on the rudders; most students are too light in the beginning. My good performance was most likely due to my prior training in soaring. In the future, while flying aerobatics in Citabrias, a Stearman PT-17, and my own Starduster II biplane, it was to be a prerequisite for handling taildraggers.

Dan and I started to fly at around the same time. He started at another airport in Pipers, and I had started in Cessnas. It all depends on whichever type you feel more comfortable with. Later, Dan switched to the same instructor I had had in the C-152s.

After logging 250 hours in the air, I was checked out in the Cessna C-172, a four-seater. Later I took lessons in a Bellanca 8KCAB, Super Decathlon. One day when I showed up for a lesson, I found the instructor, who also owned the plane, had sold it. That canceled my chances of getting checked out in that plane.

Flying down to Batavia, N.Y, I made arrangements to learn the Citabria 7GCAA, the little brother to the Super Decathlon. To fly the taildragger solo, I had to take 25 hours of dual instruction for insurance purposes. That wasn't cheap, but it was worth it for me to fly the plane. The instructor was an excellent pilot and teacher, and we had a lot of fun. Dick taught me basic aerobatics, such as snaprolls, barrel rolls, Immelmans, chandelles, loops, and spins.

Me, doing all those unusual attitudes in a plane? It was hard to believe. A few years before, I would have been too queasy watching a plane going through those maneuvers.

One day the instructor was demonstrating snaprolls. He would do one, then I would do one, and so on. I wasn't doing them just right, so we kept at it, again and again. Suddenly it hit me—I was getting sick, and fast!

"What's the quickest way down?" I asked.

"Spin!"

We were at about 4,000 feet. I put the plane into a stall, kicked the rudder over, and we came down. Leveling out at 1,500 feet, we headed for runway 28 at Batavia, and I think we were on the ground in 10 minutes. I didn't lose it, but it was close. It's like driving a car—if you're driving, it's okay, but if someone else is driving, it can make you sick.

In 1986 I had the opportunity to fly with Bill Thomas, who won a Silver Medal in the 1972 World Championships in France. He won in a borrowed Citabria, but he now instructs in a Pitts Special 2S-2B, a plane with a 15-foot wing span. Flying with Thomas in the Pitts was a thrilling experience, but my head throbbed and my stomach churned for six hours after our one-hour flight.

At least I had done what I set out to do, but I figured that at age 57, there was no reason to beat myself up every time I flew. My interest was in slow, easy pleasure flights with friends. Flying a Pitts Special is my idea of "grabbing a tiger by the tail." If I had started at a younger age and trained my body to handle that kind of flying, it would have been okay.

Actually, my purpose in learning some aerobatics was only to experience unusual attitudes in flight so I would be able to handle anything that might happen. Many airline pilots have never experienced an unusual attitude, such as flying upside down or in a spin. Having executed these types of maneuvers, I think such training makes a better pilot. Soaring is also a big factor in learning "stick and rudder" and being aware of your surroundings at all times.

LOOKING WEST

For many years I took my vacations in the spring, flying to Las Vegas for three days, then visiting in California and Arizona. My favorite Las Vegas casino was the Frontier when it was only three stories high; it had a swimming pool in the back and it was surrounded by cool green grass. The temperature was probably 10 degrees cooler there than anywhere else in the city.

The Frontier's staff had the friendliness of a small casino atmosphere. Later the Frontier was sold, and a multistoried tower was built on top. That seemed to change the whole atmosphere about the place.

Down the Strip, the Sands was another nice casino, where I began to stay most of the time. Many individual smaller motel-style units were built around the pool area. The Sands was one of my favorite eating spots, just as I had liked eating at the Frontier years before. The Sands was torn down recently to make room for a larger hotel/casino.

I always rented a car while traveling in the West so I could golf, sightsee, and go dining at places off the Strip. Red Rock Canyon was one of my favorite spots about 20 miles to the west; Bonny Springs and the Lake Mead area to the east were beautiful. Many times I saw wild burros on the road to Red Rock Canyon and wild mountain sheep near Lake Mead.

FIRST HOT AIR BALLOON RIDE

While vacationing in the Palm Springs, California area for a couple of days, I stayed at the Desert Hot Springs Spa in Desert Hot Springs. Arrangements were made to do a little hot air ballooning down in Indio, south of Palm Springs. I would get up very early in the morning, maybe 5 a.m., have a little something for breakfast, usually what I had left over from the night before, then leave in my rental car. It was close to an hour's drive, but luckily there wasn't much traffic that early in the morning.

As I pulled onto the grassy field, the balloonists would already be there and have the air bag laid out on the ground. The bag would be partially inflated with a generator and blower to start with. After that was done, the propane lighter would be ignited and tipped to the side to allow the air to be warmed, while the second person, sometimes myself, held the neck of the bag. The hot air inside the bag—or *envelope,* as it was called—was lighter than the outside surrounding atmosphere, and the bag would begin to rise vertically.

At that point, everyone was told to climb into the basket. I found out early on that if you are fairly tall, stay away from under the torch or heater, or as far away from it as possible. It gets pretty hot under there, especially on a bald head.

While I was fooling with my camera, we rose very quickly, and as I happened to look over the edge of the basket, we were already 200 feet in the air and rising. What a thrill!

There were only four of us in the basket, counting David, an English fellow, who was the pilot. We rose to 1,000 feet and found an air current that took us in another direction. Deciding to go in still another direction, David released some air from the flap at the top of the balloon to let some hot air out. We descended to 500 feet and continued to drop until we floated along and skimmed the tops of an orchard of date palms.

As we passed the orchard, we went over a farmer's pasture, and two strawberry roans were spooked by our shadow over them.

David triggered the propane torch with a good 20-second blast that sent us back up to 1,000 feet again, and we drifted in another direction. That is how a balloon pilot is able to direct his craft, by ascending or descending to various altitudes and drifting along with the wind direction. In doing that, David was quite capable of steering the balloon over a vacant field while his assistant was tracking us in a pickup truck along the side roads and communicating with a walkie-talkie.

Brushing the weeds and cacti along the ground, David continued to deflate the envelope with the top flap opened wide; then he told me to "get out." That was where I came in handy as I tried to hold the wicker basket and keep it from being dragged until enough lift from the envelope stopped it dead.

Everyone assisted in packing the envelope and basket into the truck. We all piled in and returned to our original starting site.

'HOUND AND HARE'

Two years later, at virtually the same time of year, I took another flight with Sunrise Balloons Inc. at the same place. The flight was about the same, but the pilot was not. This pilot's name was Bill, I believe, and we went up around 2,500 to 3,000 feet to find the right wind direction. We drifted around the same area as before, and after an hour we were about ready to make our landing.

Just as we touched down in a field and the envelope started to drag the basket, the pilot yelled to me, "Jump out!" and "Hold the basket down to keep it from tipping over."

After everything was under control and all the lift taken out of the bag, everyone was allowed to exit the basket.

In 1994, when I met Joyce, my second wife, I went with her and her girl friend Linda to Phoenix, Arizona to take a balloon flight. The lady pilot who was taking Joyce and Linda in her balloon announced to them that this flight would be a "hound and hare race," in which one balloon is the hare and starts out ahead of everyone else. The rest of the balloons are the hounds, and they start chasing after the hare some 15 or 20 minutes later across the desert. At some point the hare will drop a prominent marker, and as the hounds give chase, they must locate and land nearest to that marker.

Another lady balloonist was without her crew when everybody was ready to start. I had planned just to get some snapshots of Joyce taking off in her balloon, but the lone balloonist pilot, Joany, asked me if I would crew for her.

I agreed and climbed in. Off we went in the midst of some 30 balloons going every which way. That's really something to see from the ground, but it gets more exciting when you're flying in the middle of a balloon race.

I tried to keep track of Joyce and her balloon, but they soon left us in the dust. Probably the highest any of the balloons went was about 300-500 feet, and most of them stayed much lower, maybe 200-300 feet, as we skimmed along the barren desert. Joany was not greatly experienced, because we seemed to lag behind when we apparently did not pick up the right wind direction too well. Using a two-way radio, we were in constant contact with everyone else, listening to all the chit-chat of the hounds trying to keep track of the hare.

All the balloons had some kind of logo, some signifying sponsorships such as "RE/MAX Realty," "Century 21," or "Desert Buick." Others were privately owned and had their own logos, like "Marge's Baby," with a teddy bear painted on the envelope. All of them had absolutely beautiful artwork. Both Joyce's pilot and mine owned their own balloons, but for the life of me, I can't remember their logos.

After 45 minutes or so, a call came across the radio: Someone had located the marker and landed near it. The race was over, and almost everyone tried to land as close as possible to one of the dirt roads. Joany brought her ship down not too close to a road, but I guessed that her assistant would be able to get to us in a pickup truck.

When we started to land and bounce around, the wicker basket began to drag along the stones, cacti, and tumbleweeds. Sooo—guess what? Joany yelled, "Elmer, I'll need to have you jump out and hold the basket."

That was fine; there was no one else to hold it anyway.

After we secured and packed everything, all we had to do was wait for the pickup.

Traipsing through the desert, I finally located Joyce, Linda, and their pilot, a schoolteacher by profession. They were all sitting around, relaxed, as the pilot talked nonstop about her stuffed Panda bear, which she attached to the side of the basket whenever she flew.

Her assistant drove up in the pickup truck, and we all helped to load up. Then the customary bottle of champagne was opened for all new balloon passengers. Shortly afterward, we were taken back to the starting point where our own vehicles were parked.

I think what I enjoyed most about the "hound and hare" flight was the low-level soaring over the desert. That was legendary.

RETIRED FROM THE COAST GUARD, 1983

When I turned 54 in 1983, I began thinking of retiring from the Coast Guard. The luster and excitement had long since worn off.

Over an eight-year period (1965-73), the CG had taken in many individuals who rushed to sign up to evade the draft because of the Vietnam War. There were many in the enlisted ranks who did nothing but breathe when at Reserve meetings. They contributed nothing, and they had no intention of participating in anything. These individuals were there to sit it out until their 8- or 6-year obligations were over.

We asked them, "Why did you join if you did not like the Coast Guard?"

Their reply was, "Well, I had to join. I didn't want to. I had no choice."

We would answer, "You did not have to join the Coast Guard. You did have a choice: you could have been drafted."

The World War II and Korean War veterans were rapidly retiring, both officers and enlisted men. Those who were still active had already served their 8-year obligations and so were not bound but simply dedicated to the service or working toward retirement.

Many professional people were given commissions after a short period of training and did not serve a day of active service. It seemed that a large number of these were industrial-type professionals and educators. Most of them appeared to be men dedicated to the military services, but there were many individuals who were good at administrating but sadly lacking when it came to leadership and discipline.

Some of these "line officers" had what is called "small person syndrome," which means they insisted that things be done their way just because they had seniority over someone else. In other words, these so-called adults acted like "the world's oldest 10-year-olds."

In August 1983, I had taken on other commitments and interests to the point where I could not devote enough time to the Reserve program. I submitted a letter of resignation, via the chain of command, to Washington. My resignation was accepted as of Sept. 30, 1983.

My total commitment to the U.S. Coast Guard for creditable service time was 36 years, 5 months, and 25 days.

FLO'S CAFÉ

Flo's Airport Café at the Chino Airport in Riverside, Calif., is probably the most popular place in town. They serve the best sausage gravy over biscuits that I've ever tasted. Their hamburgers, served at lunchtime, aren't too shabby either.

Everyone in the café is connected, in one way or another, with flying, although there is also a fertilizer company at the airport that the local farmers patronize. The only exception is on Sunday morning when residents and visitors flock there for their weekly breakfast. I have seen 15 to 20 people waiting outside to get in for a table.

Sitting at the lunch counter over a cup of coffee, I was passing the time of day with a fellow pilot. He knew what was going on around there better than I, a stranger. We talked about biplanes, and he said, "You might be interested in visiting the Executive Hangars, where Hartley Folstad has a couple of Stearmans."

I thought that must be where those Stearmans at the Chino Air Show the year before were from. After the show that Saturday, I had taken a ride in one of them. It was really a first-class ride, especially because the pilot had let me handle the plane.

Finishing my coffee, I rushed out to the rental car and, looking 500 feet east, I could see the Executive Hangars. Driving through the gate and down between the hangars, I came to the end on the left side; that was where Folstad was located. I could see the two silver Stearmans in the hangar and an office cubicle on the left at the rear.

Parking the car as close to the hangar as possible, I went inside the hangar and over to the office. There I introduced myself and met Hartley Folstad, a senior captain of United Air Lines. He not only owns two (more since then) Stearmans but gives rides and instruction. I approached him about lessons, and he wanted me to start right away.

FLYING THE STEARMAN

We pushed one of the planes out of the hangar and into the middle of hangar row. Hartley told me to climb in the rear cockpit and buckle up. He climbed in the front and started the engine with an electric starter he had installed. Good idea, I thought. I was to find out later that not all Stearmans have such modern conveniences.

As Hartley gave the "220 horses" a little more power, we started to roll, moving between the rows of hangars, and I had to fishtail so I could see what was ahead. I was in awe of this new venture. Flying the Stearman was a great thrill for me because it was my dream to fly a biplane. The open cockpit, the smell of gas and oil, wearing a leather jacket and helmet with a six-foot silk scarf tied casually around my neck and flowing behind me—that was just about the whole scene for me. (I was to learn later that long silk scarves are not to be waved around in the air but are mostly for show on the ground.)

After a few flights of touch and go's, Hartley pulled an engine out on downwind. He yelled over the intercom, "You've lost power! What are you going to do?"

I said, "Head for the runway!" A student is always taught that early in flight training.

"You'd better head for it right away!" Hartley said, sounding a little concerned.

I thought I had time to square off my downwind to base, then to final approach, but immediately we began to sink like a rock. I had not realized that a biplane will not glide like a Cessna or a Citabria. On final approach, about 100 feet above the pasture and a herd of cattle just below us, I realized we were not going to make the runway.

Hartley took over, giving the engine full power and holding our altitude at 30 feet above the ground. Then he turned the controls over to me as we made the runway.

I learned a very sobering lesson: A biplane's glide/ratio is not anywhere near as good as that of a single-wing plane, because a biplane has flying wires and a heavy landing gear plus parts that create more drag than a conventional single-wing plane.

Later, after a few more flights, when Hartley pulled another engine out, I headed directly for the end of the runway, with no "squaring off of corners."

At about the same time I got a chance to fly in a P-51D at the Chino Airport with Johnny Maloney. That was a very dramatic event for me; I remembered those great fighters in World War II, and as a kid I would dream of being a fighter pilot in a P-51 *Mustang* or a P-47 *Thunderbolt*.

MEADVILLE AIR SHOW, JULY 1988

The Meadville Air Show in western Pennsylvania gave me my first opportunity to fly with the Geneseo Warplane Museum group. Leaving on a Friday afternoon, we were to fly to Port Meadville, attend a "Welcome Dinner" that evening, then perform on Saturday and Sunday.

My part was very small; my good friend Gordie was the Stearman pilot, and I rode "shotgun" in the front seat. The flying time from Geneseo to Meadville was a little less than two hours, and we arrived just in time for the reception and dinner. The citizens made us feel very much at home and indeed welcome.

By the time I woke up the next morning, Gordie had already left the inn for the airport to check out the Stearman. I caught a shuttle bus provided by the local air show committee and rushed out to where Gordie was "filling her up."

At every air show, the veteran pilots go out early in the morning and have a "Dawn Patrol" to check out their planes but also to "buzz" the town and wake up everyone to let them know "the flyboys are around!" I would have liked to have flown with Gordie, but he flew that one by himself.

I assisted mainly on the flight line during the air show, except when our "bird" was scheduled to fly. Gordie asked me to go with him, and I was thrilled just to be a part of the action. We flew around the "patch" (pattern) three or four times to show the spectators what a primary trainer (PT-17) looked like. Four or five other trainers, like the BT-13, a basic trainer from the museum, also performed with us.

The highlight of the show was our B-17 ("Fuddy Duddy"), two P-51s, a P-40, and two or three AT-6s dressed to simulate Japanese Zeroes, all performed a Pearl Harbor 1941 exhibition.

I usually stayed around the Stearman when we allowed the fans to walk up and touch the planes. Nowadays, most air show crowds are kept back away from the planes, but we felt the people should be able to see and feel the planes. Everyone was observed very closely, however.

While I was standing by our craft, a few men would approach me and say, "I used to fly one of those planes when I was in the Air Corps in Texas in '43," or something to that effect. With misty eyes and voices cracking, they would reminisce about the days of 45 to 50 years ago.

One man, obviously much younger, held his young son, maybe 5 or 6 years old, up to see the cockpit. He told the boy not to touch anything. I knew exactly how the boy felt, so I asked him if he wanted to sit in the cockpit. His eyes lit up and so did his father's, as I lifted him into the front seat. He was thrilled, as I'm sure I would have been if someone had done that for me at that age.

Many in the crowd would have friends or family members take their pictures standing next to the plane, and believe it or not, some youngsters wanted my autograph. Gordie missed out on that.

Sunday was pretty much the same. Each morning before the show started, there would be a meeting of all pilots and crew. Everyone was briefed on the rules and regulations, and "Safety First" was always stressed.

I didn't fly in the show on Sunday afternoon because Gordie was busy taking another passenger. After the show ended, another meeting was held by the museum members to critique the program. Changes had to be made because some pilots had to fly different aircraft back home. Gordie had to fly the P-40 back to Geneseo, so he asked me if I would fly the Stearman. I was very excited about the opportunity, and I felt 10 feet tall as I walked back to the flight line.

MY CHANCE TO FLY THE STEARMAN

Gordie cranked her up for me, and I flipped the switch as the 220-hp engine jumped to life. I knew all eyes were on me as I taxied out and departed, because I had not flown the museum's Stearman, *Solo,* yet. Although I was one of the first to leave Meadville, I was one of the last to arrive back in Geneso, our home field, because almost all the other planes were much faster.

I did take a little detour on the way home. My cousin Shirley and her husband Bill had a summer cottage on a lake not very far from Geneseo. It was on a direct line between Meadville and Geneseo, so I diverted the plane and made two passes over the lake near their cottage.

As I sighted the museum, I noticed that almost all the other planes had already arrived. Making a nice three-point landing, I taxied up to the main hangar. A group of the pilots and crewmen who had flown in before me gave me a nice round of applause. I shut down the engine, and as I climbed out, I still felt 10 feet tall. It took an hour to get the smile off my face.

Sometime later that summer, I was selected to fly the Stearman to the Oswego County Air Show in Fulton. B. J., one of the female office workers at the museum, had been selected to go as my partner in the Stearman.

FULTON AIR SHOW

Taking Friday afternoon off from work, I headed on down the Route 390 Expressway to Geneseo and the National Warplane Museum. Almost all the pilots and crew were there getting ready to depart for Oswego County Airport in Fulton. After checking out my plane and getting the word to move out, I had B. J. climb in the front and buckle up. After checking her straps, I climbed in the rear and buckled myself up.

Taking off and climbing out over Geneseo, I noticed B. J. immediately pulling something out of her leather flying jacket. For a split second, there was a blur, and then everything went white!

I had been hit in the face with B. J.'s six-foot white silk scarf, and I was fighting to get it off. I thought of setting it on fire—but I had no lighter. I thought of tying it down, around my left rudder pedal, but I couldn't reach the pedal. Then I thought of tapping B. J. on the shoulder and getting her attention.

She thought I was complimenting her on her fine selection of white silk scarves. Finally, peeling the scarf off my face for the umpteenth time, I balled it up and motioned for her to "stuff it." It was okay for the pilot flying in the rear seat to wear a six-foot silk scarf waving in the wind, but not someone sitting in the front seat.

There were no further visibility problems, and about an hour later we landed at Fulton.

A picnic supper was served in one of the hangars for the air crew and air show personnel that evening.

The Saturday and Sunday air shows went pretty much the same as in Meadville. I was solely responsible for the Stearman, and she performed perfectly.

Two U.S. Marine Corps Harriers, AV-8As with four pilots, had been invited, and they performed on both days. The Harriers were vertical takeoff and landing (VTOL) airplanes, capable of a maximum speed of 737+ mph.

On Saturday, after the pilots of the two Harriers performed their very impressive demonstration, they were invited to join the air show VIP tent. One of our NWM personnel invited the two Marine pilots to fly with two of our planes and pilots. A Marine captain agreed to fly with Bob in our PT-23, and the Marine lieutenant was invited to fly with me in the Stearman. He was very enthusiastic about flying in an old biwing, which he had never done before.

Standing on the left wing, I assisted the young Marine lieutenant as he strapped himself in. I related the old Air Corps adage given to cadets in primary training: "The Stearman has three speeds—takeoff at 80, cruise at 80, and land at 80." We both had a good laugh over that one.

Flying around the "patch" at less than 1,000 feet, I could see that my passenger was thoroughly enjoying his ride. When we taxied back to the line and shut down, he said elatedly, "That was the slowest and lowest I've ever flown."

On Sunday afternoon, as the show ended, B. J. and I departed, heading southwest for Geneseo *sans* her silk scarf.

An hour or so into the flight, we encountered rain squalls and some headwind. I tried to skirt around them, but they were too widespread. Dropping down to 1,200 feet and managing to avert a couple of thunder heads, we came out of the rain after 10 or 15 minutes. We touched down on the long grass strip at the NWM field after a flight of two hours. The splendid weekend came to an end all too soon.

July 1988: Shot at the air show in Oswego, N.Y.

OUR OWN AIR SHOW

The National Warplane Museum Air Show was in the middle of August 1988. For several years it had been scheduled for September, but the weather proved so unreliable that we changed it to the summer. It was one of the biggest shows of its kind in the country.

I worked on the flight lines both Saturday and Sunday. The museum's PT-17 was flown exclusively by the NWM president's daughter in the air show on both days. However, after the show on Saturday, one of the NWM officers told me he had a favor to ask.

We happened to be sitting in the VIP tent at the time, and he asked if I would take up some of the Army Golden Knight skydivers and let them jump.

I said, "Sure, Tex, I'd be glad to."

The Army Golden Knights had performed earlier in the show and were spectacular. These young Army jumpers had hundreds of jumps their credit, and they vied with one another to see who had jumped the most out of different kinds of aircraft. Not very many of them could say they had jumped from a PT-17 Stearman.

I met Ken High, the Army Knight, as we walked toward the Stearman. I briefed him as we climbed in and buckled up.

We taxied out to the strip and took off, circling around the airfield to 3,000 feet. As we reached altitude, Ken climbed out onto the left wing and was attempting to secure the front cushion. It seemed to float, so he tried stuffing it under the seat on the floor. That caused the stick controls to bind to the point where I could not move the elevator of aileron. (At that point, I couldn't see what he was doing. He told me this later on the ground.) Luckily for me, he changed his mind and decided to leave the cushion where it belonged and to fasten the seat belt over it.

Then Ken gave me the "thumbs up" sign and stepped off the wing backwards. I circled around to watch him for a minute, then descended back to the field. That was a first for me, and it was a strange feeling to take someone up in a plane and come down alone.

I taxied up near the VIP tent, where the second Knight, Mark French, climbed aboard. Tex buckled him in. Mark was just as eager to go as his friend Ken had been.

I took Mark up to 3,000 feet over the field, and as soon as he was ready, he climbed out on the left wing and waited for the exact spot, even though there was little wind. With a "thumbs up," he, too, dropped off—backwards.

It was a real thrill for me to take those two fellows up and let them jump.

Since that time, the museum has split into two factions, with one staying in Geneseo and the other group moving to Batavia and later to Elmira.

During the years that I was a member, I really enjoyed working on the old planes and sharing my interest with the rest of the members.

STARDUSTER II

In the spring of 1989, while visiting Chino Airport, I did not get to fly with Hartley Folstad in his Stearman because the weather was below minimums every day. I did talk with him about different planes that I was interested in buying. He said that one particular plane would be just the type for me—a Starduster.

I spent months looking for either a Great Lakes or a Starduster. Someone told me that I wouldn't be satisfied with a "Lakes" because it didn't have the power or performance that a Starduster had.

In late June I heard of a Skybolt for sale. I checked it out and thought it was a nice plane after I flew it, but the front cockpit was too small. If I were to give rides, it would have been very hard for the average person to climb into and out of.

In early September I found the ideal plane, a Starduster II, a two-seater (tandem), open cockpit, taildragger. She had a 180-hp Lycoming engine with a wingspan of 22 feet (top) and 15 feet (bottom). The fuselage fuel tank held 27 gallons, and the top wing held another 14 gallons. A clear plastic canopy slid forward to cover both the front and rear cockpits for flight.

I purchased the plane in Canada, which meant that the FAA required that it be inspected, and a qualified pilot would have to fly 40 hours off it before I could legally fly it.

I had met Brian Liley sometime before when he was teaching a stall, spin course in his Aeronca 7AC Champ. Brian was an Eastman Kodak pilot and an excellent instructor. He offered to fly off the required hours for me. Another good friend, Earl Luce, helped me and advised me on improving the Starduster. We flew together in the "Duster II" many times and in his little 65-hp Cubby.

When I first bought the Starduster II, it landed "squirrelly." Brian said, "You really have to stay on top of it *whenever you land*. It wants to turn sharply to the left, all the time." Yet on taxiing and takeoff, the plane went straight down the runway.

This became such a topic of conversation among the "weekend warriors" (a group of private pilots at our little airport who met every Sunday to swap and tell flying tales) that they gathered around my plane, trying to solve the problem. Each and every one of the 10 had a different opinion.

I stood back and let them swarm like a bunch of bees as they discussed the problem. They were pretty sharp men, and I was sure they all meant well, but I'll bet maybe only one or two had ever flown a biplane, or taildragger. They were all tricycle-type landing gear pilots, which is vastly different from handling a taildragger.

Just then, Earl Luce came up to my hangar, where everyone was gathered. They were all busy talking at once, with no one listening to anyone. Earl called me aside.

"I know how to solve the problem," he said, "and I can prove it as soon as these fellows leave."

August 1993: Showing my grandson Jim the Starduster II.

Some of the fellows had little use for Earl because he probably knew more about planes and flying than they, as "oldtimers," knew. He belonged to the local chapter of the Experimental Aircraft Association, of which he had been president for years, and had successfully built and flown three home-built planes.

Earl's diagnosis on the Starduster II was that the main gear was out of alignment, so when the others had left to swarm around someone else's plane, he and I went to work.

Two 2x4s 12 feet long and a 25-foot tape measure proved that the main gear was perfect. Earl said, "Then it has to be the tailwheel."

As luck would have it, Brian Liley flew in with his *Champ,* and we discussed the problem with him. Brian said, "Let's go. We'll take my tailwheel off and put it on your Starduster."

We put the *Champ* tailwheel on my plane, and Brian flew it, doing a few "touch and gos." He couldn't wait to shut down on the ramp as we ran to him. "That's it!" he exclaimed.

I ended up buying a new Scott Model 3200 tailwheel, but it was well worth it. They listed for $600, but I got a good deal—$300. Next, I had to buy new bungee cords for the main gear. One mechanic said he could put them on in probably less than a day. Another mechanic's plan was to grease large metal plates, assuming we could find them, to slide the wheels together for some reason or other.

Earl said, "Elmer, meet me after work, and we'll take off the old bungees and put the new ones on and be home in time for supper."

Earl had a come-along, which we rigged from the hangar's rafter. We lowered the come-along's hook from the rafter straight down through the front cockpit to the landing gear and lifted the plane. We cut off the old bungees and put the new ones on—in 20 minutes! We were both home an hour before supper. It was all well within conformance to FAA rules and regulations and approved by licensed inspectors.

Earl seemed to have endless ideas about how to improve, redesign, and build airplanes and a few retrofits on some, too.

FLY-IN AT PENN YAN

In May 1992, I went back to New York for the summer and kept my Starduster at a grass strip on a farm near the village of Hilton. Earl Luce had told me about it; it was where he kept his Cubby; Ward Wolf owned the farm and kept his Cessna 172 there in a hangar, so he allowed me to tie my plane there too.

The strip was 1,200 to 1,300 feet long, depending on whether the grass on the west end was cut. I loved it because, coming in from east to west, there were two 80-foot trees just far enough apart for a plane to slip between them. Then you had to straighten out and drop in, already 200 feet past the runway from the east. The Starduster stalls at 72-75 mph, which gives the pilot no more than 1,000 feet to roll out. Actually, there was plenty of runway for the plane to come to a halt without using brakes, but it kept things interesting.

I attended many fly-in breakfasts that summer, along with Dan, but mostly with Earl. Those fly-ins are a lot of fun, especially when you enter the airport traffic area. There may be 20 planes in the local area, all circling, entering the traffic pattern, some with radios and some without, and all different types of planes. The situation makes for some interesting maneuvers, all of which demand extreme caution.

One of my favorite spots for fly-in breakfasts is the Penn Yan Airport in the Finger Lakes region. It's situated at the north end of Keuka Lake (shaped like a Y) and makes for one of the prettiest cross-country flights from Hilton or Brockport, N.Y.

As Dan and I arrived in the area, I observed eight planes in the pattern for "28" (runway) and another four or five off to the north and east, approaching.

That airport always has a fly-in to commemorate the Fourth of July, and it is always well attended. They always seem to have great weather ordered for the occasion, too.

Looking down on the scene, I could see that already there were 40 to 50 planes lined up in rows, parked in the field on the north side of the runway. A line was queued up for breakfast, snaking its way from the main hangar, past the steel-drum band from a local high school, and on out into the field for at least 300 feet.

I thought, *Wow! There won't be any pancakes left by the time we get on the ground.*

I watched for an opening and entered the "patch" (pattern) down-wind at a 45-degree angle, falling in line behind three planes ahead of me that looked to be Cessna 150s or 152s, two-place high wings. My Starduster had a higher "stall rate" than the Cessnas, so I had to make a little wider pattern out to the right so I could keep behind them.

Approaching "base," I swung a wider pattern to allow plenty of time for the planes just ahead of me. Turning on to "final" (heading for the runway), the last plane ahead of me was just short of touchdown, and as we continued to descend, I slipped the left wing to hold my direction and lose more altitude faster. We dropped in with a three-point landing that would not have awakened an insomniac. I felt satisfied, and even Dan gave me a "thumbs up" from the front cockpit as we rolled down the runway to turnoff.

The grounds crew directed us to taxi between two rows of planes, and after passing several, we were directed to park as I applied more power, holding the left brake and swinging the "Duster II" around to line up.

I couldn't wait to get in line because I was hungry and it was probably 11 a.m. by then. First, however, I had to make a pit stop; my kidneys are good for maybe an hour or two when flying.

While I was standing in line, all the time smelling the aroma of hot pancakes and spicy hot sausages frying and knowing I was still half an hour away from eating, a fellow airman struck up a conversation.

"How far can you fly your biplane without having to land?" he asked. He had seen us coming in on final approach and landing.

"I can fly it at about 120 mph for an hour or so," I answered.

"Well, that's not too great for only 120 miles."

"It's not the plane," I exclaimed, "it's my *kidneys!* I have to come down every hour or so for relief."

The steel-drum band sounded great, as they have other years. We passed them as the line started to move again. Entering the large hangar, I started looking around the vast throng of aviation enthusiasts and be gan to recognize familiar faces as they tried to catch my eye and give me a hearty wave.

"There's Brayton and Barb," said Dan pointing out a couple from the old, now defunct Hilton Flying Club. Dan and I were probably the newest and last members.

Near them was my old friend, Mac McGrath, and his wife Annie. Mac and Brayton were both World War II Army Air Corps mechanics. Mac was very interested and quite adamant about "annualing" my Starduster when I first bought it. I was very fortunate to have found someone like him to work on it.

Finally getting our pancakes, sausages, juice, and coffee made for a Chinese balancing act as we tried to wend our way through the maze of long tables and folding chairs to find a couple of vacant spots. Going through a trail like that makes it seem as if there is no sober pilot in the whole building. I would much rather go through a couple of barrel rolls and chandelles in the air.

Hearing someone calling my name, I turned around to see Brian Liley, an Eastman Kodak corporate pilot who had recently put me through his "Stall/Spin Course" in his Aeronca Champ. What a fun course! I thoroughly enjoyed every minute of it.

Jimmy Sample and his father, "Crazy Charlie," were nearby; both of them are excellent pilots from Kendall, N.Y.

After finishing breakfast, almost everyone gathered around in small groups to check out different machines and their equipment. Occasionally there might be a couple of twins (two-engine), and sometimes there might be two or three biplanes.

As things wound down, pilots and planes started to clear props, start up, taxi out, and depart. Dan and I climbed in our plane and followed the crowd. When the runway was cleared, the go-ahead was given to cross over, and we fell in line on the grass taxiway along the south side of the runway. In my taildragger, I couldn't see ahead of me at all, so I had to fishtail, back and forth, looking out of each side of the rear cockpit.

After a short runup and check of all systems, at the end of the taxiway we were ready to take the runway and depart the airport pattern to the west over the north end of Keuka Lake.

CANADA, BY MISTAKE

One fine day, sometime later, Earl and I decided to fly to Three-Mile Bay, northwest of Watertown on the New York sectional chart. I was flying, and Earl was supposed to do the navigating, so, departing Ward Wolf's Lawton Road strip, we climbed to 2,000 feet and flew east along Lake Ontario. When we were in the Rochester air space, we had to drop down to 1,700 feet, and after leaving it, we climbed to 2,500 feet.

Soon we were flying over the beautiful lush cherry orchards and farms. It's impossible to get lost in that area of the state. I was thinking, *You have the lake on the left, and on the right you have bays, inlets, main roads, and what all.*

Next we spied the tall towers of Oswego, then, passing south of the city, I angled more to the north-northeast. Leaving the shoreline, we passed over Mexico Bay as I climbed to 3,500 feet and headed for Sandy Harbor. We flew north along Route 3 between the lake, still on our left, and Route 81, the Northway Freeway, on the right.

We started to pass over some bays and inlets as I tapped Earl and pointed down.

"Is that it?" I asked.

Earl shook his head and yelled, "No!"

After another couple of bays and inlets, I asked Earl, "Are we there yet?"

Again he turned and shook his head. "No."

Then, passing over a fairly large island, I looked ahead and saw a large city with high stone or brick walls along the water.

I tapped Earl and asked for the chart as I gave him the stick control. One quick glance told me—we were in *Canadian air space!*

I abruptly took the controls again and did a 180-degree turn, heading south over Wolfe Island and looking fro the St. Lawrence Seaway— south channel.

I dove through the broken clouds and headed east when I saw a large ship in the channel. Flying farther, I saw a water tower, so I dropped down to 700 feet and spotted the Clayton village water tower, with its name on it.

I got Earl oriented on the chart; then we headed for Three-Mile Bay and Don Lance's farm and airstrip.

When we got on the ground and shut down, Earl and I had a good laugh.

"Both of us can fly," I told him, "but I'd better navigate and let you fly from now on!"

I must go down to the seas again, to the lonely sea and the
sky,
And all I ask is a tall ship and a star to steer her by,
And the wheel's kick and the wind's song and the white sail's
shaking,
And a grey mist on the sea's face and a grey dawn breaking[*]

—John Masefield

RETIREMENT FROM GM

In January 1991, I was looking forward to retiring in five or six months. Sometime in February, I read a magazine ad saying that the Merchant Marine was acutely short of radio officers for their ships, which had been recommissioned for the war in the Persian Gulf.

I immediately contacted a Mr. Rae Echols of the American Radio Association (ARA), a union for Merchant Marine radio officers. He indicated that they were desperately short of ROs for their ships.

Replying to his questions, I told him that I had had my 2nd telegraph license for the past 37 years and was ready to use it. However, I couldn't go to sea until I retired from Rochester Products, a division of General Motors.

I completed a mountain of paperwork, such as fingerprint checks, Coast Guard license, mug shots, passport, military service history, company résumé, and personal recommendations, all of which had to be signed and notarized before sets of copies were sent to various addresses. The process took several weeks, and as time went on, I got more and more excited about going back to sea. I knew I'd like it, because it had been my dream when I was young. I found it hard to believe that I was finally going to have the chance to do it again.

----

[*]From "Sea Fever" by John Masefield.

During lunch period at work, I asked a friend, Marty Elliot, an amateur radio operator, to make me some Morse Code tapes at various speeds so I could build up my speed. It took no more than a week or so to get my speed up to 30 wpm.

Rae Echols called me every week with a list of ships he had to staff with ROs and said he wanted me on the staff list. I had to remind him that I couldn't go until I retired from GM at the end of June.

Surprisingly, I never gave as much thought to retiring from GM as I did to going into the Merchant Marine in June. Some fellows I knew at GM would count the years, the months, and finally the days they had left before they were going to retire. I never thought too much about it until I had a goal to shoot for: a chance to start a new career.

ME, A DRUG ADDICT?

One of my last requirements before going into the Merchant Marine was to take a drug test. The week after the test, the laboratory in San Diego called. One of the doctors wanted to speak with me.

"Mr. Walters," he said, "you failed the drug test." Before I could register disbelief, he continued. "Looking at your forms, I don't believe that you take drugs; most likely you never have. However, I must ask some questions. Do you like bread?"

"Yes," I replied.

"If you like bread, do you like rolls? Maybe those rolls with poppy seeds on them?"

A little perplexed, I answered, "Yes, I like them. In fact, I had some—probably within a week or two before the test."

The doctor sounded relieved. "That answers one of my questions. Now, do you drink once in a while?"

"Sure," I admitted, "I have a drink every so often. Maybe a vodka martini or a gin and tonic."

"Okay," said the doctor, "you've answered all my questions. You failed the test because the poppy seeds and juniper berries (gin is made from juniper berries) showed up as heroin and cocaine in the drug test. What may surprise some people is that traces of poppy seeds or juniper berry extract may stay in a person's body for some period of time. Under these circumstances, I'm happy to say that you passed!"

I was flabbergasted by what the doctor told me. I told my friends at work and others in Hilton; they all laughed and thought it was hilarious. Anyone who knows me knows that I wouldn't even take an aspirin for two weeks before a drug test.

On the last Friday in June 1991, I retired from General Motors after 20 years and 5 months. I could have worked for many more years, I suppose, but my goal had always been to retire at age 62. My philosophy was, "If you don't have it made by now, you never will."

The old gang in the Electronics Repair Shop gave a little party in my honor (probably glad I was leaving). One of the most thoughtful gifts they gave me was an old life preserver full of bullet holes, for use in my new career. That was meant as a joke—at least, I thought it was.

The following Tuesday, with tickets provided by the ARA, I flew to Washington and took a cab to the Sparrow Shipyard outside Baltimore. There, my assigned ship, the *SS Pride,* a C-3 cargo ship, was tied up and being loaded with shoring material.

SS PRIDE: THE MERCHANT MARINE

A third mate showed me to my stateroom, which was actually a passenger's cabin. It was located two decks above the main deck, portside, forward.

After stowing my gear away, I went out and met the other radioman, Rich, and together we went up to the Salon, where the previous captain was being relieved and the new one was assuming command.

The new captain checked our credentials, then dismissed us. The relieved captain told us there were some thieves aboard because someone had stolen the 24-hour clock from the radioroom. Rich and I went to the radioroom immediately and saw that the clock was indeed missing.

Agreeing that we needed a clock for exact time in the radioroom, we approached the new captain (Jake) and told him we would have to go ashore to buy a new clock. We called a cab to pick us up.

Just as we were about to go down the gangway, one of the seamen said, "Hey, you two are the radiomen, aren't you? The old captain just left the ship with the radioroom clock in his baggage!"

Talk about thieves!

Two days later, on July 9, 1991, we departed at 1600, headed for the Persian Gulf. We cruised up north of Baltimore, then through the Delaware-Maryland Channel, down Delaware Bay, past Cape May, NJ, and out to sea. Our heading was to take eight days to Gibraltar.

The *SS Pride* was formerly the *SS MorMac Pride* (of Moore-McCormack Lines), which sailed from East Coast ports to South Africa. Her radio call was WMDV.

The ship had 23 crewmen and 12 officers. The food was very good. There was always a good selection at every meal. Fruit and juices were available in the refrigerator at all hours, and you could always make a sandwich if you were up late at night.

As we left the East Coast, Rich, as the senior radioman, had his choice of watches. At first he said he wanted the morning watch, but then he changed his mind. He wanted me to take the morning watch so he could sleep in all morning.

It made no difference to me; I was happy to be sailing and operating a radio again. I took the AM watch and had the PM watch off.

I was amazed to see that Rich spent a good half of his afternoon watch lying out on deck. He seemed to feel no obligation to his duties.

I had suspected from the first couple of days that someone was on drugs. Rich was the so-called "senior" radioman because he had made a previous trip. He had the radio officer's stateroom, located near the Bridge. I had a passenger's cabin down a deck or two below. That was fine with me, because it was larger than the officers' staterooms.

When my watch was over, it was a chore to get Rich out of his stateroom for his watch. I had to rap on his door several times because he was hard to arouse. Finally he would open the door a crack; he always kept his room darkened, and there was a sweet, sickening smell that constantly permeated his room.

The sea was a little choppy, but not rough, crossing to Gibraltar. After five days of sailing, we entered the brightest, bluest water I had ever seen—the Mediterranean Sea.

July 1991: Here I am in the Radioroom of the *SS Pride* (WMDV), a C-3 cargo ship, formerly a Moore-McCormack cargo-passenger liner. I was the radio officer on a trip to Ad-Dammam, Saudi Arabia during Desert Storm and Desert Sortie, July 2 to Sept. 5, 1991.

TRANSITING THE SUEZ

On July 22 we arrived at Port Said, Egypt, and the next day we transited the Suez Canal. Going through the canal, each ship is required to have a pilot and eight line handlers—for what, I don't know. The Suez is a big ditch dug out of the desert sand. There are no locks to raise or lower the ships to different levels. I don't recall any lines needing to be handled. These eight "handlers" came aboard and immediately began to lay out their wares to sell to crew members.

They had little trinkets, T-shirts (Egyptian cotton), papyrus (paper) prints of Egyptian art, turbans to wrap around your head if you wanted to look like Yasser Arafat, and maybe some discount watches. They lay about all day, and at the end of the Canal they disembarked in their linehandlers' boat and left.

The Canal pilot assigned to our ship kindly told the captain that, for his services, he would need 36 cartons of American cigarettes.[*] The captain told him in plain English to "Go to hell!" but he gave the pilot 12 cartons, which was about 11 more than I would have given him.

The first thing these "pilots" do when they come aboard is report to the Bridge, then high-tail it down to the officers' dining room and order a huge meal. I have seen them wolf down enough food for three starved stevedores.[†]

Halfway through the Canal, we entered a large basin or lake where the North and South Convoys pass. The North passed first, then the South. Before going through the southern channel, all the ships in our convoy would be assigned a priority.

The Canal pilot on our Bridge notified the captain and Rich that at 1120 local time, the Canal Authority would call every ship to pass information on 425 Khz. (Radiotelegraphy).

Rich got very uptight because he was very poor on Morse Code; he barely passed his 2nd Class Radiotelegraph Test. He had just relieved me of my AM watch 15 minutes earlier, when he came down to the dining room to see me. I had just ordered my noon meal. He said he wanted me to take over his watch so I could get the message from the Canal Authority.

"Sure," I said. "That's no problem; I've handled important messages in the Coast Guard and never got overly excited about them."

---

[*] The pilots are paid by the Canal Authority, which collects huge sums for ships passing through as it is.

[†] Years later, on a German freighter passing through the Panama Canal, I saw a Panamanian pilot doing exactly the same thing in the dining room.

I left my dinner on the table and went back up to the radioroom, arriving just as the Canal Authority was starting to send its message over the radio. It said:

```
Ships will go as follows BT:* NR1
HERIOT NR2 USNS MCCANDLESS NR3
TRUETT NR4 USNS PRIDE...
```

As they called our ship, I turned on the transmitter (set on 425 Khz.) and answered with my handkey, "de WMDV R TU," which meant "This is *SS Pride* Roger thank you."

That was all there was to it. Our ship was #4 in sequence going through the south channel. Rich ran up on the Bridge and passed the message to the captain and the pilot. They probably thought he was a very efficient radio officer.

He came back to the radioroom, and I went below to finish my dinner.

Exiting the Canal, we continued into the Red Sea and proceeded southbound. This area was very hot and humid. On July 26, we left the Red Sea and headed around the Arabian Peninsula and into the Indian Ocean, where we encountered some stormy weather, No. 4 seas with large swells.

We then passed through the Straits of Hormuz and north into the Persian Gulf. The U.S. Navy had done an excellent job of clearing most of the mines out of the Gulf by that time.

---

* BT means "break between sentences" in Morse Code.

SAUDI ARABIA

We sighted Ad-Dammam at about 2000 and anchored out. The ship always had floodlights shining into the water when anchored, so there was plenty of light. Looking down alongside the ship, I saw an occasional water snake about 6 feet long with black and yellow rings around its body. They are very poisonous. The Persian Gulf must be full of those creatures!

The next day we entered port and tied up at a pier where there were other American C-3s—the *SS Gibson* and the *SS California.* The *California* was leaving, heading east via the Indian Ocean and the Pacific to San Francisco.

For the next three days and nights our ship was loaded with Army fuel tank trucks, huge generators, two-wheel trailers, Humvees (a new military personnel vehicle), and 4-ton trucks.

A dark gray cloud cover hung over the entire Middle East area, caused by the oil well fires in Kuwait. That was an eerie sight to behold when, at high noon, the headlights on all vehicles had to be turned on.

The crews of all the ships were restricted from going ashore and roaming about on the base. Three of us did go ashore around 2000 one night, for a half-hour, to a little café near the pier. As I recall, we each had a Coke and a lambburger. It wasn't too bad. In fact, I rather liked it because I like lamb anyway.

The next day, Aug. 4, we departed the pier and anchored out about 2 miles to take on "bunkers." That means we were refueled by a barge. Leaving there that evening, we headed south, and the next day we passed through the Strait of Hormuz. Iran was in sight in the East, and Oman was in sight in the West.

SOS DE WMDV

On Aug. 7, at 0835, the *SS Pride* lost power; "the fires went out." Somehow water had been pumped into the fuel tanks, and the fuel-water mixture was not volatile enough to burn in the boilers.

At that time we were about 50 miles off the coast of Oman. Ten minutes later we had lost power on all equipment. Another 10 minutes and the emergency power was intermittent on my radio equipment.

The captain told me at lunch that we would have to send an SOS in a few minutes. Our position was 17 deg 26 min north and 56 deg 20 min east.

I said, "Captain, all emergency power for the radio transmitting equipment is off. I have no power."

"I see," he replied. "We'll use R/T (radiotelephone) on the Bridge."

By 1200 hours we were still foundering 8 miles offshore. My receivers were working because they require much less power than a transmitter. I could hear other ships calling one another about our predicament.

The captain had sent a "MAYDAY" at 1230 local time on radiotelephone. The *SS Cape Catoche*/KPLF was the closest ship, steaming toward us, but she was not expected to reach us until 1700. That ship was handling all our radio traffic, too.

At 1430, the *SS Pride* was drifting perilously close to shore, maybe 1-1/2 to 2 miles from the rocky cliffs of Oman. The barren terrain was mountainous, and the coastline was rocky shoals. If we had to take to the lifeboats, we didn't know what to expect.

Then, only half an hour later at 1500, the fires were lit, the engine started, and we began to pull away from that ghastly coastline. A few minutes later, after we were sure of power, I sent a message to KPLF, *SS Cape Catoche,* thanking the crew for watching over us and telling them that we would no longer require their assistance. It was a comforting feeling, knowing that I had full power on my radio gear.

Over the years I have wondered how many radiomen had to send or were directly involved in an SOS their first time out. Years before in the Coast Guard, I had worked distressed vessels, but never at the distressed end.

Passing along the southern coast of the Arabian Peninsula, we entered the Gulf of Aden, and some hours later we were back in the Red Sea. Heading north one morning, we were buzzed by a USAF C-130.

The Air Force flies patrols up and down the Red Sea to check all shipping coming and going to the Persian Gulf Theater of Operations.

SHOPPING FOR 'GOLD'

We anchored out in the harbor of Port Suez for 8 or 10 hours. A few of us went in a motor launch to the pier and caught a cab for the best hotel in town. After a couple of beers, I joined up with a third mate and two engineers for dinner at the hotel.

We ran into Rich and one of his friends. They wanted me to join them; they were going into town where the shops were located. I wanted to see if there was anything worth buying in the shops.

I asked what they were shopping for.

"Gold," Rich said.

I thought about that for a while, and suddenly it hit me—how naive could I be? Gold, my eye! They were asking for drugs in all the shops, not a doubt in my mind. Luckily, they found none. I hate to think what would have happened if the three of us had been arrested in Egypt. Muslim countries have very strict drug laws.

We caught the launch at the wharf late at night and got back to our ship. Early the next morning the ship weighed anchor, and we moved out to transit the Suez Canal.

SUEZ

Some unforgettable sights along the Suez kept me busy shooting video when I had time. A large concrete structure, probably 150 feet high and 50 feet on each side, was a monument to the defense of the canal during World War II. During the 1967 war between Israel and Egypt, the Israeli Air Force made Swiss cheese out of almost all buildings along the canal, but this monument was only pock-marked.

As we cruised up the canal, I noted a stark contrast from one side to the other. The west bank has lush green fields or orchards that are obvi ously irrigated. The east (Sinai) side is nothing but sand; not even a weed is visible.

We saw different types of ships in our convoy and passed a variety on the high seas. The SL-7 Rapid Deployment ship is used by the military to move equipment fast to a battle site. This ship is capable of cruising at 45 knots through the water, and it churns up a "rooster tail," which is impressive.

Another ship, the "Ro-Ro," called "Roll-on, Roll-off," is capable of extremely fast loading and unloading. I saw one in Charleston, S. C. that unloaded in one 8-hour shift. In contrast, our C-3 cargo ship, *SS Pride,* would require 3 to 4 days to load and 2 to 3 days to unload.

Farther up the canal, there is a palatial mansion that was used as a summer home by one of the Egyptian presidents. It is a very large white house, with probably 15 or 20 rooms. The grounds are well manicured with gardens, shrubs, and palm trees all around the property. This home stands out because there is very little else in the area to attract attention.

Exiting the canal at Port Said, we cruised for 5 days westward through the sparkling blue Mediterranean.

GIBRALTAR

On Sunday, Aug. 18, 1991, the ship dropped anchor off Gibraltar to take on fuel (bunkers). I secured the radio watch at 0900.

At noon, the captain asked where Rich was. I replied that I had no idea, but I knew that Rich had gone ashore with a couple of his buddies on the first motor launch at 10 or 11 a.m. They were going "shopping."

The captain said, "Well, you'll have to stand his watch until he shows up."

I was sure the captain had finally figured out that Rich had gone ashore. Even so, I stood the R/T watch on the Bridge until 1400 when it was secured.

At about 1600, I went ashore in the launch. The captain was on the same trip, along with 8 or 10 others. It was a little comical, the captain sitting in the back of the launch by himself and everyone else crowded up front away from him. I decided I would talk to him about it later at the end of the cruise.

As we came to the pier, I spied Rich walking toward the launch. He saw the captain, so he ducked out of sight until everyone went by. As I was walking down the street a few minutes later, he caught up to me. Evidently he and his buddies had not found what they were looking for, so he decided to join me. He thanked me for covering for him earlier.

It was Sunday, and almost all the quaint little shops were closed. I was still able to buy a few postcards.

That evening, Rich and I had a very nice dinner at the Holiday Inn. There weren't very many other places we could find that were decent. I honestly believe that was the best dining Rich had ever experienced. He had come from an Indian reservation and had been quite poor when he was growing up.

Back on board the *SS Pride,* at 0500, I conducted the predeparture tests of the radio equipment, which are required before leaving every port. We weighed anchor an hour later.

BACK HOME

The voyage across the Atlantic was uneventful. We arrived in Charleston, S.C. on Aug. 26, 1991. The *SS Pride* tied up at an Army pier, and I secured the radio watch.

One of the things I missed most while at sea was a newspaper. Believe it or not, listening to newscasts at sea is not the same. I was starved for a good old American newspaper. The next morning after breakfast, I left the ship and walked and walked—it must have been 3 or 4 miles—to a small crossroads store in the country and got a newspaper. I think I even bought two different papers to read.

We were going to be in port for 4 days, so I took a cab into Charleston for the day. I especially enjoyed the flea market and farmers' market.

WORLD'S OLDEST 10-YEAR-OLD

On Aug. 30, we departed in the afternoon and sailed up the coast, bound for Norfolk, Va. I was taking some video shots from the Bridge wing. The captain had seen me shooting videos before, so he asked if I would like to get some shots from the Bridge, early in the evening.

"Yes, sir, I'd be glad to," I answered.

One of the third mates near me spoke in a low voice. "You're in for it now, Sparks."

"Why? What do you mean?" I asked.

"The old man—Jake! He's going to eat that up. When you come to take those shots on the Bridge, he'll love all that attention. You watch— I'll bet he has his uniform on, too."

It was our last night of sailing, and what a beautiful evening it was! The seas were calm, and there was a warm breeze coming offshore.

The evening meal finished, I went up to the Bridge with my video camera, and—surprise, surprise! There was our captain, all decked out in his dress whites, short sleeves with the 4-stripes and white shorts. His fat belly had such an overhang that it was impossible to see his belt buckle.

This fellow was probably 15 years younger than I. I was 62 and the oldest man on the ship. The captain was grossly overweight, and the way he devoured popcorn, candy, and Coke every night, it would be a miracle if he lived to 55!

Afterward, he mentioned that he would like a copy of the video, and I said I would be glad to send it to him.

Throughout the entire two-month trip, I had found the captain very cold to me personally. I was never able to strike up a conversation with him. He would give only a curt or terse reply to all my overtures.

One evening after we had been to sea for two or three weeks, some of us gathered in the salon for the after-dinner movie. Of course, the movie never started until the captain arrived and got situated in his favorite seat up front with his popcorn, candy, and Coke.

A captain deserves and demands respect. I have never been disrespectful of a captain or any superior in my employment history.

Capt. Jake sat down and began small talk before the movie. Looking straight ahead, he asked, "Where did you say you're from?" No one answered. He half-turned behind him to his left toward me and asked again, "*You!* Uh—where did you say you're from?"

"Captain, are you talking to me?" I asked.

"Yeah!"

"Captain, I have been on this ship for over three weeks," I said. "My name is Walters, but *you* can call me *Mr.* Walters. I'm from Rochester, New York."

"Yeah, okay," he said.

End of conversation. All 12 officers had known my name within three or four days. The captain addressed all the others by their first names in conversation, in the dining room, or wherever. Eventually my patience wears a little thin, and I feel that I should be accorded mutual respect like any other fellow human being.

One of the engineering officers once said to me, "We don't have much use for the captain. He's very immature and unsure of himself. I think the problem he has with you is that he's intimidated because you're older, more mature, and more sure of yourself."

I felt a little sorry for the captain. I dislike using a trite phrase too much, but this one fit him: the world's oldest 10-year-old!

DECOMMISSIONING

There was a beautiful sunset as we began a left turn toward Chesapeake Bay that evening. The next day we entered Norfolk and tied up at a pier in the shipyard.

On Sept. 2, 1991, the crew was discharged from the ship. The captain called each man individually, paid him off, and gave him a discharge slip. We were then free to leave.

Rich was one of the first to leave in the morning. The captain called a cab for Rich and paid his fare to the airport. That much I know because I helped Rich carry his bags to the cab at the foot of the gangway.

At around 1500, I was discharged by the captain. He did not volunteer to call a cab for me or anyone else, except Rich. I suspected there was some collusion between the two of them. Maybe there had been more than one officer who "smoked" on that trip!

Leaving as soon as possible, I called my own cab and went to the Patrick Henry Airport. Taking a Piedmont plane to New York, I arrived in the early evening to catch a USAir to Rochester and home that evening.

I spent the next two months working on my own plane, getting it annualed and flying along with my good friend Earl. I visited friends, and in early November I left for Las Vegas for the winter.

Spending six months in Las Vegas proved to me that the winters there are colder than I thought they would be. The temperature there often falls below freezing, and I like shirtsleeve weather. I did do some flying there to pass the time. I checked out in a Piper Cherokee 140 at Sky Harbor Airport in Henderson. I really enjoyed low-altitude flying over Jean Lake, which is a dry lake bed.

BACK TO SEA AGAIN

By January 1992, I was getting itchy to sail again, so I called the ARA office, which is now in Phoenix, and asked for another ship. Two weeks later I had my assignment and headed for Long Beach, California.

The ship was a 665-ft tanker, the *OMI Hudson.* Reporting on board, I was introduced to Capt. Johnson and the other RO, Jon from Salt Lake City. A young fellow, he was very sharp and knew radio operation. There was certainly a world of difference between him and that other RO, Rich. Jon was very helpful at all times.

The ship departed Long Beach, and we headed for the San Francisco Bay area, actually Concord, where we took on a load of gasoline. Concord was a familiar place to me because I had been there twice to attend Coast Guard schools.

After two days of loading, we departed and sailed under the Golden Gate Bridge as we charted a course for Panama.

I stood one-man watches for the entire trip because Jon oversaw all operations. He spent most of his time working on his laptop computer. Much of the radio equipment was different from that on the *SS Pride.* It was newer and all in working order.

For instance, if a crewman wanted to make a telephone call home, all he had to do was go to a booth outside the radioroom and, by dialing, make contact by satellite with the States, then go through landline systems. On the *Pride,* a crewman had to come into the radioroom and, at the convenience of the RO, the R/T would be set up through satellite to the States, then through landline.

On the *Hudson,* we had a weather fax machine that gave a surface analysis display, sea state forecast, and a satellite photo of cloud definition, outlining continents and islands within range and showing the earth curvature. These maps were all very helpful to the Bridge for navigation.

The voyage from San Francisco to Panama took about 7 days. It was great to be back at sea, especially in the sparkling blue Pacific, where I've sailed mostly. The ocean was calm, the sky clear, and the weather mild all the way.

1992: TRANSITING THE PANAMA CANAL

Arriving in Panama, we anchored out until early the next morning, when the ships lined up to enter the canal. Each ship is assigned a priority, and the *Hudson* was one of the first. Someone told me once that cruise ships are always given priority to go ahead of other ships. That is not true, because both times I've gone through, a cruise ship was behind us. This time a Caribbean cruise liner brought up our rear.

The day started out rainy and cool but cleared by 1200. Transiting the canal takes about 10 to 12 hours from Balboa to Cristobal.

Leaving the east coast of Panama, we set a course past the Cayman Islands and west of Cuba. Our destination was originally New York with a full load of gasoline. As we approached the east coast of Florida, a radio dispatch came in from the company's headquarters. The message stated that we were to divert from New York to Jacksonville, Fla.

On Saturday and Sunday, Mar. 14 and 15, we were discharging the entire load of fuel from one of the fuel docks on the fringes of the city.

On Sunday, Jon and I took a cab into the newly renovated Jacksonville waterfront with many pedestrian areas, boating docks, and unique storefronts. This was an entirely different city from what I had seen when I left the Coast Guard boot camp 45 years earlier. All I saw then was the train station.

After three days, we left Jacksonville and sailed down around Florida, past the Dry Tortugas and New Orleans, up the Mississippi River. About 75 miles from New Orleans, we arrived at Plaquemine, swung around in the river, and tied up on the west bank. There is a large chemical plant where we spent a little less than a day, taking on caustic soda.

It was fascinating to watch other boats going up and down the river. Large freighters were heading up toward Baton Rouge or farther, and some were wending their way back down to New Orleans and out to sea. Many barges, sometimes 5 or 6 of them, were being pushed upstream by a tug to other unknown destinations.

When I was a kid, I wondered about tugs and boats and ships: where were they going and what was their cargo? Now I was standing on a ship and watching all this activity on "Ol' Man River," and I was still wondering.

Plaquemine is just 10 or 12 miles south of Baton Rouge, and there are many chemical plants along the river. A lot of cotton is grown there, too.

Besides caustic soda, we also took on a shipment of benzene and cruised on down the river toward New Orleans. In the late afternoon we passed the city, noticing familiar places I have seen many times over the past 40 years. Farther down we passed through the Delta and went out through the Southwest Channel into the Gulf once again.

The next stop was Galveston, through the Galveston Bay and up the San Jacinto River to Pasadena. After two more days of loading caustic soda, we continued down the Texas coast to Corpus Christi. A day later the ship departed for the Panama Canal and the West Coast.

The meals on this voyage were excellent. We had a good selection, and everything was well prepared. I remarked to the head cook one day, "Cookie, this is the best food I've ever had on a ship."

I have forgotten his name, but I do remember that he was from the Cayman Islands. Many men from the Islands go to sea as cooks. Their fathers and uncles before them had done the same. It's a tradition for them.

The cook eyed me suspiciously and said, "You know, Sparks, I've never gotten a compliment from a radio officer before. You guys always complained about the food. You're the first RO that ever complimented me."

"Well," I said, "I'm telling you, this food is like a banquet. You're not a cook, you're a *chef!*"

He gave me a big smile, and I think I made a friend for life. But it was *true.* I learned years ago in the Coast Guard to make friends with the cook and not to complain. When I was a boot seaman on the *CGC Unalga,* I once complained to the cook about the food.

He said, "You don't like the food? Don't eat it."

It was as simple as that.

MY LAST MESSAGE

On April 1, we again went through the Panama Canal and proceeded north, QRD (destination) Long Beach.

The first or second day out of the canal, when I tried to send the daily Position Report message to the ship's company headquarters, I had a problem raising anyone on the air. Finally, using radiotelegraphy on 500 Khz, I contacted NMG, Coast Guard Galveston Radio.

That was the last message I sent. Shortly after that, radiotelegraphy became a trade of the past. The 500 Khz International Calling and Distress Frequency was secured and replaced by the Global Maritime Distress and Safety System in 1993. It felt good to think I had worked the Coast Guard first in 1948 and for the last time in 1992, a span of 44 years!

Two days after our arrival in Long Beach, I signed off the ship and returned home to Las Vegas on Good Friday, 1992.

I had made two voyages in the Merchant Marine, and I could have stayed on indefinitely. I opted to call it quits because I had accomplished one more dream of my youth. The first voyage was an ego trip, and the second, totally unplanned, was to prove to myself that I could still handle it after all those years. I figured that at my age I didn't need to continue sailing. I wanted to move on to other things.

XV. ENJOYING LIFE

Going back out West in November, I was determined to go farther south than Las Vegas. I spent the winter of 1993 in Bullhead City, Arizona, which proved to be much milder and warmer than Las Vegas and about 120 miles farther south.

Through my sister, Gin, I was introduced to a great couple who had been retired from Eastman Kodak for several years. Madge and Harold Reed took early retirement and traveled west to settle down in Bullhead City in the mid-1960s.

We three became very good friends over a few short years, and I love them dearly. Practically every year the Reeds go to Mexico for a month in the winter, and they love it down there. "?Que pasa, por aqui," Harold!

While in Arizona during the late winter, I drove through Lake Havasu City, which is 40 miles south. I liked the place so much, I decided to build a house there. It seems to be a well-laid out city with homes in a wide price range, quality schools, beautiful churches, and fairly good stores for shopping. The city has a well-balanced economy, with light industrial manufacturing, services, and a healthy retiree populace. For that very reason, there are good medical facilities available.

I have fallen in love with this city for all its attributes, not the least of which is its flawless weather. Even sunny California cannot claim better weather.

MARRIED AGAIN

In late February 1994, I met someone who completely captivated all my thoughts, dreams, and feelings from then on.

I had met Joyce Switzer-Nairn in Lake Havasu City while she was visiting friends. Nine days later I asked her to marry me so she wouldn't have time to think it over.

She is Canadian, from St. Marys, Ontario, and lost her husband, Don, in October 1991. She has three grown children: in birth order, Gary,

Randy, and Nancy. Gary and his wife Marlene have four children: Jeff, Jillian, Ian, and Adam. Randy and his wife Lisa have two: Brandon and Kyle. Nancy and her husband Dale also have two: Corey and Devon.

Our wedding took place at Joyce's old homestead, which Gary and Marlene now own. We were married in the front yard, among the flowerbeds and huge shade trees, on July 2, 1994. About 75 friends and relatives were there. My daughters Deborah and Dorothy were there, the latter with her husband Chris. My son Dan, his wife Beth, and two sons, Ricky and Jim, also attended.

Mrs. Elmer D. Walters: My wife, Joyce Irene Switzer-Nairn Walters. We met in February 1994 and were married five months later.

Something I never thought I would do was drive a farm tractor. Joyce gave me a half-hour lesson, then let me go to it. I loved it! I have soared and I have flown airplanes upside down, and this was yet another thrill. Gary trusted me to cultivate a 100-acre field, and my first thought was, how am I going to turn this big machine around 180 degrees in that field? The 30-foot-wide cultivator looked 100 feet wide to me.

I got too close to a hedgerow one day and pulled up a 30-foot tree, about 4 in. in diameter at the base. Wondering what to do, I thought for a minute, then raised the forks and freed the tree. The next year I was not asked to help; I think I was on probation after the tree incident. But in 1997 I was called back again to fill in. That made me feel much better.

June 1996: Cultivating on the farm in St. Marys, Ontario, Canada.

SECOND HOME IN CANADA

Joyce and I had a new home built, just a quarter of a mile down the road on one of her farms. We spend the months of May through October there; from November through April, we're in Arizona.

The only traveling we did our first winter together was to fly home to Canada from Arizona for Christmas and New Year's. In February 1995, we flew to St. Petersburg, Florida to visit relatives and toured the Cape Canaveral area. We also attended the annual Hilton, New York reunion of transplanted family members, which was held at Sawgrass Park in St. Petersburg.

XVI. SPACE-A ADVANTAGES

During March 1995, Joyce and I thought we would like to see the Hawaiian island of Kauai. We departed from March AFB, California, in a KC-10, a version of the DC-10. A comfortable 5-hour trip took us into Hickam AFB, where we stayed at Oceans Resort. This fine hotel is only two blocks from Waikiki Beach, and we get unbelievable retired military rates. The Hale Koa, a large hotel then being built for military families only, was not completely finished.

As I found out later, there are other places to stay that are much more reasonable and closer to Waikiki Beach. Every time we go to Honolulu, we favor Oceans Resort. The rooms are comfortable, and they have good service, excellent meals, and free parking.

KAUAI

After sightseeing around the city and taking a bus tour of the island of Oahu, we decided to check out Kauai. We bought an island tour of Kauai that included airfare and an 8-hour bus trip. The woman at the tour office put me in charge of making sure that everyone got on the right flights and were accounted for until we got back to Honolulu later that evening. Keeping track of 50 or 60 strangers at the terminal certainly made the waiting time seem shorter.

"How can I do this?" I asked Joyce. "Some of the people are going on one flight, and the rest of us are going on the next flight to Kauai. I don't know just how many there are, and none of us has name tags or any identification."

Part of the group went by Hawaiian Air, and the remainder flew by Mahalo Air. The Mahalo Air flight took about an hour. The tour bus driver/director met us at the air terminal. Starting our tour, we drove along the south coast where all the flowers seemed to be in bloom. Kauai is called the Garden Island, but it seems to be as much a "flower island" as Maui is.

Traveling farther, we climbed up the Waimea Canyon Drive to the top. The view was spectacular from there, like a miniature Grand Canyon with lush vegetation. We heard "cluck, cluck—peep, peep, peep" all around us, and the tour director explained.

"During the last hurricane we had, the chickens were blown from sea level up to the top of the mountain here, and they have survived and multiplied in the area now. They seem to be wild, because no one has claimed them."

As we descended back down to sea level, we drove along the coast until we came to the "Spouting Horn." That is where the surf comes in and blows the seawater up through lava tubes. The water blows up 10 to 15 feet in the air, like a whale spouting through its blow hole.

After finishing lunch at one of the island's championship golf courses, we continued through Lihue and up the eastern coast to the Wailua River. The boat trip up the river displayed beautiful cliffs with heavy foliage.

Hiking up the path through the dense jungle from the boat wharf to the grotto, I kept glancing through the trees for breadfruit in the area. I saw none, although the guide mentioned that there was some there. I had been fascinated by breadfruit after reading stories of Captain Cook searching for it in the South Seas. Later I was to find breadfruit in Pago Pago.

The Fern Grotto was a hauntingly beautiful cave, luxuriantly festooned with large ferns.

We were pleasantly entertained by a young man playing a Hawaiian guitar and a young lady dressed in a sarong and singing Hawaiian songs, which everyone enjoyed very much.

We were waiting for a return shuttle to Oahu, so to finish out the last two hours, the tour director/driver thought we would all be interested in Lihue's shipping docks and warehouses. Most of us slept through it until we were taken back to the airport. A tour around the little city observing all the beautiful flowers would have been much more interesting than the warehouses and docks.

GUAM

Returning from Kauai, we stayed at Ocean Resorts for another day, then returned to Hickam Air Force Base. Checking the board or TV screens, we saw Guam on the list, and it looked appealing. The flight was due to depart in a few hours, so I signed us up. It was a civilian charter, DC-9, bound for Guam and on to Kadena, Okinawa.

It was a first-class flight; the rear of the plane had standard airline seating, and a cabin attendant served regular hot meals. No box lunches this time! The front half of the plane carried freight, and the passenger section was at the rear. It was an 8-hour flight, passing over Midway Island.

"Hafa Adai"—"Welcome to Guam," the large sign at the Anderson Air Force Base gate says.

We checked in at Space-A lodging for a room. The accommodations were just like a good motel. Walking back to the AMC terminal, we rented a car, which is really necessary to get around in, even on the base.

The next day, Joyce and I headed southwest toward the capital, Agana. The city is populated with Japanese, so I'm told, and has many Japanese-owned hotels. They are all expensive, because the Japanese like to come down there from Japan for vacations. Others usually avoid that area.

Motoring along, we continued past the city and along the west coast to the invasion beaches of World War II. A very impressive memorial to all the armed forces is located there. It brought back memories of where my brother Harvey landed as a Marine. Our two cousins were there, too.

We passed along the U.S. Naval station; there also is a U.S. Coast Guard base that controls all the Marianas. Nimitz Beach is there, and farther down is Mt. Lamlam, the highest point on the island at 1,334 feet.

The little town of Umatac marks the landing of Ferdinand Magellan in 1521 with a monument in town. We passed through and continued up the East Coast back to Anderson AFB.

Joyce and I enjoyed playing golf at the Palm Tree Golf Course on the base, soaking up the beautiful scenery and looking as far as the eye could see out to sea.

We spent time on the Anderson beaches on the North Coast, where the white sand stretches out of sight. There are beautiful cocoanut palms along the beach where we had lunch on some days.

Flights came in periodically from Japan or Korea, destined for Hawaii and the mainland States. As we checked the AMC Terminal board, it might show an in- or outbound flight from Japan to Hawaii. Some travelers might be irritated, hoping to catch a flight, only to find out hours later that the mysterious flight had been canceled.

Joyce and I learned that you have to be "flexible." If you normally try to keep a schedule—and some retirees do—you should forget it in this part of the world. You must learn to relax and "go with the flow."

On that visit to Guam, we went back to the terminal three days in a row, only to be turned down; on the fourth day we finally caught a flight to Hawaii. While waiting, we worked a lot on our golf and spent a few hours each day on the beach.

Returning to Hawaii, we got a flight back to March AFB the day after, and finally reached home in Arizona.

MAUI

Because we were captivated by the irresistible charm of Hawaii, Joyce and I decided to return in April to see yet another island, the beautiful "Valley Isle," also known as the "flower island"—Maui.

Catching a "hop" via a C-141 from March AFB, California, we landed at Hickam Field on Oahu after a 5-hour flight. After two days at Waikiki, we made travel arrangements for Maui. An hour's flight by way of Hawaiian Air led us to Kahului Airport. Picking up a rental car, we drove directly to the east side of Kahului on the water. The motel accommodations had been made from Honolulu, but the motel unit was somewhat below our standards. A window was broken and had fallen out, so we contacted the management, and they moved us to a much better unit. You wouldn't believe it was the same motel.

Later that afternoon we drove in to Lao Valley, where the park is enchantingly serene. The unusual rock formation is called Iao Needle, where there is a rushing water stream flowing down the mountainside.

The next morning we viewed sugar cane fields and pineapple fields on Route 30 as we headed for Lahaina. In Lahaina, we visited many shops and watched the boats that were coming and going in the harbor.

Kaanapali Village was where we arrived for lunch. We ate in an outdoor area with tables and umbrellas right in the main section. After lunch we toured the shops and the Whalers' Museum. We drove on along the west coast as far as Kahana. On the return trip, there were several wayside parks with beaches for suntanning or swimming. Then we stopped to visit the Maui Tropical Plantation. There were many products, connected mostly with pineapples or macadamia nuts, on display. Trees that are native to the islands are grown there and on display.

The Plantation regularly puts on a *luau* for tourists, and we were tempted to stay for it, but we had a previous engagement for the evening, so we continued back to our motel and later went out to dinner.

The next day after breakfast, we planned to head east on the Haleakala Highway to Pukalani Village, then on a narrower road climbing up to Haleakala Peak. With beautiful clear skies all around us, we snaked our way up the winding, twisting road as we met many cyclists on their way down. There must have been 100 or more; they ascend the peak in vans, autos, or trucks, then cycle all the way back down, maybe as far as Pukalani, a distance of 26 miles.

The House of the Sun Visitor Center is at the summit, where the wind that day was blowing 35 to 40 mph and the temperature was 45 degrees. It was quite a difference from the 75 degrees we had enjoyed an hour or two earlier at breakfast.

The scenery was breathtaking as we scanned the colossal Haleakala Crater to the east. The crater measures 25 square miles, and there is a 3,000-foot drop from the top of the rim to its floor.

As we surveyed the area to the south, the sparkling blue Pacific could be seen from only six or seven miles away. That area was called the Alenuihaha Channel, and the little isolated island of Kahoolawe could be seen to the southwest.

Leaving the summit, we started our descent, and there was almost complete cloud coverage around the south, west, and north sides of the mountain. The clouds were at about the 6,000-foot level, and as we drove, we had to down through clouds to maybe the 4,500-foot level.

Motoring south to Pukalani, we turned toward Kokomo and onto the northern seacoast road (Route 360), which head toward Wailua and Hana. This is the Hana Highway, a narrow two-lane road that runs along the north coast. Often we approached a horseshoe curve and bridge that narrowed down to a single lane. Oncoming traffic came to a halt, and the first vehicle proceeded across the bridge as the second car yielded. We must have crossed 30 or 35 of such areas as the road wound alongside the cliffs above the seacoast.

We drove as far as Wailua and had lunch there or in Keanae, then decided to return as we twisted and turned our way back the way we had come.

Upon returning to Honolulu via Hawaiian Air, we reflected on the few short days we had spent on Maui. It truly is a beautiful "floral island" but also is richly infused with history and evidence of whaling days, missionaries, and plantations.

It was only a short taxi ride from Honolulu International Airport to Hickam AFB, where we were able to register at Space-a-Lodging. Registering for lodging on the base is usually hard to do, but this time we were lucky. After a stay of two days on Oahu, we caught a "hop" back to March AFB in Riverside, California, and then it was a five-hour drive back to Arizona.

SPACE-A TO EUROPE

In August 1995, while passing through the Niagara Falls Air Reserve Base from our home in St. Marys, Ontario to Rochester, N.Y. to visit my children, Joyce and I decided to check on any available flights to Europe. One showed up on the board in the Ops Center for Ramstein, Germany. We had taken many Space-A journeys from the West Coast toHawaii and Guam. We had seen how the system works, but there are some small disparities among the Air Mobility Command terminals.

Niagara has no such AMC terminal; therefore, you just sign up, get on the list, and hope that the flight is not canceled. Available seats on a plane are determined solely by the pilot for whatever reason he decides on the number of passengers he wants to take on a flight.

It was mid-August when, on an early Saturday morning, we checked in at the Ops Center and were met by the Ops personnel. We observed that there were about 30 reservists and five other couples (retired military) going on that flight.

No box lunches were supplied on the flight, which took Joyce and me off guard. We had never even considered the possibility that lunches might not be available, so we scurried around for some food in the small Ops Center coffee room. I think we found only peanut butter crackers, chocolate chip cookies, and a couple of sodas for the eight-hour flight to the Azores.

Making small talk with various individuals as we milled around, we gravitated toward two other couples. They seemed to know more of what was going on because they had done this before.

The 914th Air Reserve Wing was flying a C-130A turboprop that Saturday to Lajes AFB, Azores, for overnight and refueling, then to Ramstein, Germany on Sunday.

During the eight-hour flight to Lajes, we had a chance to chat with Marge and Bill Jakes (major, U.S. Army, retired) and Esther and Jack Robson (captain, U.S. Navy, retired).

Marge, I believe, felt sorry for us because the four of them had brought a banquet for the flight. She offered us some vegetables and fruit, which was greatly appreciated. (Those peanut butter crackers did get pretty dry after a while.)

We three couples got to know one another on that flight, and we struck up a lasting friendship.

Bill and Marge rented a car with Jack and Esther upon arrival in Ramstein to tour Germany—at least that was their plan. We later found out that Jack's father had died suddenly, so he and Esther flew back to the U.S. on a commercial flight.

One couple deplaned in the Azores to spend some time there. Others went their own way throughout Europe.

Joyce and I took day trips in the area for a week, including one that was a Rhine River cruise. Cruising up the river, south to north, we visited two small villages and went into the quaint shops. Then we toured Berg Rheinstein to see a castle. We had to climb a few hundred old stone steps from the main road to the top, where the castle is, at least 500 feet above. From that astounding spot we could see shipping coming and going for miles and miles on the river. No wonder those castles were built for their vantage points.

Most of the castle was vacant, but a small part of it was inhabited by its current owners. It seemed to be in good shape considering it is hundreds of years old. Some of the rooms had tapestries and coats of arms hanging on the walls. I almost expected to see a knight in armor come charging through the large 12-foot-tall wooden door.

As we finished the tour, our hosts served coffee and cake (at a price, of course); then we started our descent down that multitude of steps.

Resuming our river cruise, we passed Koblenz, viewing probably eight or ten castles from a distance. Joyce said, "Elmer, you should get all this beautiful scenery on your camcorder. You can get good close-ups of the castles."

"You're right," I said, "except for the fact that I left the camcorder on the bus, which we won't see until we get picked up this evening." We had to make do with snapshots on Joyce's camera.

Reaching our northernmost point, Boppard, we switched to a southbound boat and headed down the river along the east shore where most of the vineyards are. Many castles dot the east shore, such as Burg Katz and Burg Gutentels. Arriving in Rudesheim in the early evening, Joyce and I chose an old-world beer garden for a couple of beers and dinner. We arrived back at our quarters in Landstuhl in the early-morning hours.

The next day I was talking to an Army sergeant about sightseeing in the area. "Trier is highly recommended," he said, "and well within a day's visit."

We found the railroad station in Landstuhl, where we were amazed at the German agents speaking fairly good but broken English. They explained the ticket system and how to find our way to Trier and back. The trains were known to be very efficient and reasonable in cost.

As we passed through the pine forests, heading west, the train arrived at the highly industrialized city of Saarbrucken. There it wended its way through the beautiful mountains west of the Rhineland. Joining the Mosel River, we snaked along the banks to pass through many little archaic villages, which made us want to stop and visit them all.

Arriving at Trier, one of Germany's oldest cities, Joyce and I were taken by its beauty. *Porta Nigra* (the Black Gate) was part of the wall that once encircled the city, which the Romans built in 400 A.D.

The Roman Imperial Baths, built in the early 4th century by Constantine I, were among many other attractions that were not to be missed on this walking tour. The Basilica, where Constantine I held court, and the Amphitheater, built into the old Roman walls, are the oldest structures, dating from 100 A.D. To actually see all these ancient buildings was mind-boggling. Pressed for time, we touched only lightly on all the sites, then had to catch the train for the return to Landstuhl.

On Friday morning we checked the AMC Terminal monitor and found a flight to RAF Mildenhall, U.K., which is near Cambridge. These flights are called MEDIVACS; they transport military patients on a regular schedule. The C-9 is a military version of the commercial DC-9. Quite often, space is available on these flights, and the service is very accommodating, such as offering hot meals during the flight.

As we left the ground from Ramstein, it was announced over the loudspeaker that the plane's mission had been diverted first to Aviano, Italy, then to England. That meant only a two- or three-hour delay in arriving at Mildenhall, so we enjoyed the scenery over the Alps, Austria, and Italy.

In the late afternoon we set down on "merry olde England," the home of some of my ancestors. The weather was very warm, about 75-80 degrees, which is above normal for that time of the year.

On Sunday, we took the base bus 70 miles into London. From a double-decker tour bus we saw the main area, including Westminster Abbey, the London Bridge (the original London Bridge is in our hometown, Lake Havasu City, Arizona), the theatre district, the Tower Bridge, and many other landmarks.

After lunch, we were viewing Buckingham Palace from the black iron gates in front when an Englishman, a very friendly chap, with his lady friend, offered us two tickets to join them in touring the interior of the palace. He had tickets for another couple who failed to show up. He wanted to treat us and refused to take any money for them. I think the price was around $16 to $18 in American money. The palace belongs to British citizens, but Queen Elizabeth II charges her subjects to see it.

Almost two weeks after arriving in Ramstein, our tourist group met again for the trip back to the States. One couple spent their entire two weeks in the Azores. Two other couples visited England and Ireland, separately. Bill and Marge Jakes spent their two weeks in the Bavarian Alps and Austria.

We were all surprised, some not too pleasantly, to learn that we would not be able to take the same flight and crew back to Niagara. The flight was overbooked with military personnel wanting to return to the U.S. on Labor Day. Joyce and I had long since understood the system and learned how to "hang loose." Some of the first-time Space-A travelers found it hard to believe that they could and would be "bumped." The military is Category 1, and the retired military is Category 6, way down the list.

Some of the retirees found their own way eventually, either on "hops" to other less desirable destinations in the States, or they ended up flying commercially.

Bill Jakes and I decided to wait it out, and the very next day the four of us caught a C-5A *Galaxy* from Ramstein to Dover, Delaware via Iceland. There again there was a pleasant surprise, for Joyce and I had never before been to Iceland.

After arriving in Dover, the four of us flew commercially from Philadelphia to Buffalo on USAir. A reasonable cab trip to the Niagara Falls Air Reserve Base got us to where our cars were parked, the end of a pleasant journey on which we made new friends and saw places we hadn't seen before.

XVII. ON THE MOVE

It must have been in February 1995 that Joyce and I had decided on a one-month tour of the South Seas and Australia.

Months later, in December, we left Las Vegas for Los Angeles on United Airlines. Later that evening, the flight headed for Hawaii, and after a two-hour layover, we flew on to the Fiji Islands. Arriving there in the wee early-morning hours, we were met by Susan, the Globus Tour guide, and the other 14 travelers on the tour.

"Kia ora!" ("Good morning!" the natives greeted us every morning.

Spending three magnificent days in the Fijis included a *hangi* (Maori dinner, or *luau*) and the Maori cultural experience, a splendid concert, *poi, haka,* stick games, and traditional chants.

On to New Zealand for nine fun-filled days. On the second day some of us went sailing in the Auckland harbor, called "the city of sails." We had dinner at a private home and got to know the people for an evening's experience; then the next day we visited the Rotorua Mud Pools and the glow worms underground. During a visit to a sheep ranch, we learned about the many different sheep, such as the Merino, Suffolk, Drysdale, Southdown, Hampshire, and more. The young fellows there demonstrated shearing the sheep and put one of their well-trained sheep dogs through its paces.

Nestled among 17 snow-capped mountain peaks is Mount Cook, where we flew into a small airport and stayed at a ski lodge at its base on Christmas Eve. This area is called the Southern Alps.

A few days later, upon arrival at Queenstown, the entire group, except for Joyce and me, took a boat ride up a river to a sheep ranch. We decided to stay in town and see the village. We soon noticed some people paragliding from the top of the mountain, soaring over the harbor and village, and landing in the local schoolyard.

"I want to do that!" Joyce exclaimed excitedly. "Let's do it!"

"Okay, let's go," I said. We were just about reading each other's minds.

An hour after making arrangements, we were on the Skyline Tram with our two young pilots carrying their packs. When we got to the top (Skyline Restaurant), where our tour group was going to have dinner that evening, we had to climb another 600 feet or more up a steep slope. Hanging onto the trees at times, we made it to the very peak, where there must have been 15 or 20 people with their rectangular paragliders, ready to soar off the mountain.

Hans, my pilot from Switzerland, said, "Okay, Elmer, when I say 'run,' you *run!*" He strapped me in first, then buckled in right behind me. The paraglider is like a high-performance parachute and is very maneuverable.

"Run, Elmer, run!" yelled Hans, and I started running for the edge of the mountain.

What is this? Am I crazy or what? I ran out of ground and I was treading air! I am scared to death of heights, like being on top of a tall building or looking over the edge of a canyon, or, for instance, going up that Skyline Tram just a little while earlier.

Probably five or six times I had taken the outside elevator at the Fairmont Hotel on Nob Hill in San Francisco, and each and every time I could not look over and down for more than a split second as we were going up. I was literally pasted to the back wall of the elevator, and I very graciously motioned to the other spectators to go ahead of me so they could have an unobstructed view.

But when I'm airborne, I have no fear—flying, soaring, ballooning, or in this instance, paragliding. It seemed that my fear on the edge of that mountain changed instantly to a calm feeling when my feet left the ground. I will admit that hearing Hans behind me had a calming effect to a certain extent.

As we sailed away from the mountaintop, I looked back to see Joyce and her pilot, Peter, just stepping off the peak to follow us.

Later, when we rejoined our tour group, Paul and Anna from Indianapolis and Claudius and Kirsten, the couple from Germany, related how much fun they had had on their afternoon boat trip and at the sheep ranch. They felt rather sorry for us because we had decided to stay in town and see the sights, until afterward when the entire group asked us what we had been up to.

"We visited the shops first," Joyce began, "and then we saw some young folks paragliding over the village, so we investigated where they were landing, and after talking with them a little while, we decided we had to do that."

I could tell by their expressions that some of them were envious. They had gone to a sheep ranch (which all of us had seen previously) and had not tried something new, as we had.

Flying to Hobart, Tasmania, we toured the unique island some 200 miles off the southern tip of Australia. We visited a former penal colony the British had used to ban those of their fellow countrymen who were thieves or murderers in the 1800s.

When we arrived at Melbourne, I bought Joyce an opal necklace and laso opals for my two daughters and two little granddaughters.

After two days, we flew to Ayer's Rock via Adelaide. Joyce and I chartered a Cessna 172 four-place plane and went sightseeing around Ayer's Rock, the Olgas (another rock formation), and Lake Amadeus.

In Alice Springs, we met Aborigines and observed how they lived. The native women cooked "witchity grubs" (about the size of a man's thumb) over an open embers fire, and some of us were brave enough to sample the roasted grub.

The food was good, but I could not convince Joyce to try it.

Riding a camel was an exhilarating experience once I shifted gears and got into "drive," but I'll take a horse and saddle any day.

There are 25,000 or more camels in Australia. The first ones were brought over from Saudi Arabia years ago for transportation across the broad expanse of the continent, and naturally they multiplied.

The hot and humid city of Cairns was our next central location for the Great Barrier Reef, which we visited the next morning, swimming, snorkeling, or just viewing the many colored fish on the reef.

One of the most spectacular rail trips in the world is from Cairns to Kuranda, which winds its way through sugar plantations and jungle foliage with native shrubs, ferns, and flowers.

We attended an Aboriginal dance theatre production, which featured the magical, mystical, hauntingly beautiful sounds of the *didgridoo,* an Aboriginal wind instrument.

Stopping off at Tahiti for a few days was a welcome rest. We flew in to Papeete, took advantage of a lovely beachside resort, witnessed the black sand beaches, toured the decidedly French territory, sampled the local fish dinners, and attended an evening's entertainment of song and dance.

That concluded our one month of touring the islands and the subcontinent.

QUICK TRIPS

In April 1996, Joyce and I drove up to Las Vegas to try our hand at the casinos for the evening. Usually we stayed on the Strip, but this time we stayed downtown at the California, off Fremont Street. No luck, of course, but we had fun.

My brother Harvey and his wife Beth invited us to visit with them, so we drove north to Salt Lake City, arriving at their home there in the afternoon.

Harvey has had numerous strokes, but he is able to get around on a walker. Beth tends to his needs and is an excellent cook.

Leaving Salt Lake City the next afternoon, we drove west on I-80 toward Reno and stayed at Battle Mountain, Nevada. It's a picturesque little town, and after an excellent dinner at one of its cozy restaurants, we tried our hand again at some slots in a casino.

What can I say? We haven't won Lotto either.

Driving on the next day, we arrived at Travis Air Base near Fairfield, California. I checked the board for flights to Hawaii. There was one, but it was full. There was a flight the next day, Sunday, so we stayed over and waited.

I got in line for the Space-A call-up, and it was no problem making the flight. I checked our bags, paid for our box lunches, and we sat downs to wait. We left on a C-141 around 10 a.m. and arrived at Hickam Air Force Base in Oahu at about 12 noon or 1 p.m. Hawaiian time.

As soon as we walked into the Air Mobility Command Terminal, we checked for outgoing flights. The monitor showed, among other flights, one to Guam, which seemed the most appealing. Having been there the year before, we had become enraptured with the island.

Eight hours on a C-141 brought us to Hafa Adai once again. Guam is just 13 degrees north latitude and 144 degrees east longitude. It is the United States's westernmost territory and commonly known as the "Gateway to Micronesia." The island is approximately 30 miles long and 8 or 9 miles wide. With its tropical humidity tempered by the prevailing winds, the temperatures are in the 80s year-'round. It is conducive to peaceful relaxation and a far cry from the commercialism of much of Hawaii.

Although I have already mentioned the importance of being flexible, this time we were planning only a week's stay. Joyce and I always try to get back to our home in St. Mary's, Canada, by May 1. Because we needed a little time to pack and "button up" things at the home in Arizona, we figured we should leave the Pacific area in 8 or 10 days.

On the first night there was no space available at the Anderson Lodge, and no rental car available, either. One of the natives, Joey Roberto, who worked for the U.S. government and had flown in from the mainland States with us, offered to take us to a good local hotel. His wife and two children came to pick him up at the Terminal in their car. We piled in back with the two little kids and our three bags, and off we went.

Guamanians are very friendly people, and they are 100 percent American. They love the U.S. and are very much a part of the States in all ways.

The next day, Joey came to pick us up and take us back to the AMC Terminal. I am proud to call him a good friend.

I picked up a rental car, if you could call it that. It ran, but that was about all. The car had numerous dents, creases, scratches, and bullet holes (at least that's what I called them). I really didn't care because I wasn't planning on entering it in a car show anyway. All I needed it for was to tool around the island, sightseeing. That car was the biggest "sight" of all.

Talking with one of the Air Police at Anderson, I inquired about his German shepherd dog, a beautiful and well-trained animal.

"Does your dog sniff for drugs on the base, Sarge?" I asked him.

"No—well, yes, partly," he answered. "His main job is to sniff out and kill snakes, brown snakes that are poisonous and have infested the island. They stowed away on some ship's cargo that came in from the Philippines some 25 or 30 years ago. We have to be careful, though, because some of the dogs like to eat the snakes."

He added that that was why there are no songbirds on Guam. The snakes have cleaned them out.

After Joyce heard that, I didn't expect her to force me to pull over when she felt like running into the jungle foliage, shaking trees for papayas or mangoes. We didn't see any snakes, and we sure didn't want to.

The incident reminded me that when I was 14 years old and in the ninth grade, our science class was studying snakes. We had a glass aquarium (without water) with maybe five or six snakes, and every day for a week or so we would discuss one of those creatures. The science teacher would select someone to get a snake while he talked about it, and later someone else would be selected to take it back to the aquarium.

On the last day I was called upon to get the last reptile, the largest one, of course. It looked about 6 feet long (actually it was only 2 feet), and it could have been a pit viper or a python as far as I knew, but in reality it was a garter snake. I reached in and grabbed that sucker, and the darned thing bit me on the left hand between the forefinger and the thumb.

Man, I didn't waste any time taking that wiggling thing up to the teacher. I was sure glad to get rid of it of that snake and sit down.

The science teacher was a good instructor but a little odd. He wore "Coke bottle" glasses and still couldn't see too well, and sometimes when we kids would take insects or bugs to his home (he lived in the village) to find out what they were, his wife would have to tell him what he was looking at. A year or so later, he left to teach at another school, and by mixing up some chemicals, he blew up the science lab. We called him "Buck Beaty."

Back on Guam, the Palm Tree Golf Course was Joyce and my favorite links on the island. The course overlooks the cliffs on the east side of the island. We played a couple of times that week and spent a lot of time on the sandy beach at Ritidian Point, the northernmost tip of the island.

One night we had accommodations at the Navy Base because we did sightseeing around the southern part of the island. I wanted to check out the Coast Guard Base located near the Navy Base on the western side. They gave me a first-class tour of their operations. That base is the headquarters for the Marianas Group, which includes Rota, Tinian, and Saipan. Joyce and I haven't yet visited those last three islands, but we certainly plan to the next time we go back to Guam.

That Friday, we were playing golf in the afternoon, when all of a sudden there was a roar of jet engines. We looked up in time to see a plane banking to the east and climbing out. It appeared to be a DC-9, probably heading for Hawaii. An hour later, after we had finished the game, we hopped in our renter wreck and went to the Terminal to check things out.

As we were watching the screen, one of the personnel asked if we were looking for a flight to Hawaii. I said, "Yes, we are."

"That's too bad," the clerk said. "An unscheduled flight came in three hours ago and refueled. They departed about 4 p.m., with available seating, but not too many people knew about it."

"I knew it!" I said. "We missed one!"

That proves that you must be ready and available, but there's not much you can do when there is an unscheduled flight. Thankfully there aren't very many.

The first thing Joyce and I do in that situation is to take a coffee break and decide what we are going to do next. So, later, we went out and had a good dinner that night.

The next afternoon, a C5-A *Galaxy* appeared on the screen. It was due in at 4 p.m. and departing around 11 p.m. for Hawaii, with maybe 65 seats. Everyone wanting to go would be covered on that flight. We all kept our fingers crossed that it would show up on time, and it did.

We left around midnight, and we all settled back to catch a little sleep on board. The military dependents with small children were just getting comfortable when the C-5 seemed to be running erratically, changing engine speeds and doing different maneuvers. Because we had been in the air only 20 minutes, the crew decided they had a problem and returned to Anderson.

All passengers had to deplane, reenter the Terminal, and wait while the flight and ground crews worked on the problem. We were kept informed about what was going on.

It was about 2 a.m. when we were told to go through the checkout again, and we then piled into the shuttle bus that takes all passengers to the waiting planes. Military planes are usually a good half-mile or more from the Terminal. Even so, the bus ride may be as much as two miles in length because the driver has to observe all the traffic patterns on the ramp. Sometimes you wonder if he actually knows where he's going.

There is no doubt in my mind that all the Air Force personnel are professionals. The shuttle bus drivers are very courteous and ready to assist at all times.

Around 2:45 a.m. we left the ground again, destined for Hickam Air Force Base in Hawaii. The flight continued without incident, and upon our arrival we made provisions for lodging at the Pearl Harbor Submarine Base BOQ.

Later the next day we caught a C-141 for Travis Air Force Base, where we picked up our car in the fenced-in security area and drove some 600 miles back to Lake Havasu City.

In late April we closed the house for another hot Arizona summer (in late June 1994, the temperature hit a record 129 degrees) and checked to make sure the bubbler system was operative for the bushes and trees. I summerized by MG *Midget* too. We set the security systems, locked the doors, and left.

HOME IN ST. MARYS

The spring and summer in southern Ontario were pleasant. I put in a vegetable garden, mostly for something to do and to watch things grow. I enjoy giving almost all the vegetables I grow to friends in St. Marys and even took some back to Dot and Dan in New York.

In early August, our good Space-A friends Bill and Marge Jakes came for a short visit. Joyce and I enjoyed their company, and we relished showing them the beautiful farmland around Ontario. The Amish in the area were cutting hay at the time, using their teams of horses with mowers; the men and boys pitched the hay up onto the wagons.

Shortly after that, our dear friends from Bullhead City, Arizona, Madge and Harold, arrived for a short visit. We delighted in showing them much of the same area. St. Marys has an excellent small-town restaurant, formerly Sir Joe's but now called Damen's. Whenever someone comes to visit, relatives or friends, we enjoy taking them to that restaurant for dinner. They always have a great buffet, and the lunches and dinners on the menu are superb.

Our favorite place for coffee and breakfast is the popular Sunset Café. Almost every day we go in there for coffee and meet many of the local townspeople for a little chitchat.

Braden, an enterprising young man, has done much to build up his business in just a few short years.

After morning coffee, LeRoy, Don, Big Bill, and maybe Doug or Bob usually leave the counter and find an out-of-the-way table where they can be heard exclaiming: "Pass!"— "Pass!"— "Clubs are trump!" Then one trick, two tricks, three tricks and *"euchre!"*

If one of them is not there, there is always Graf to fill in for one of the empty chairs.

St. Marys Station, Ontario, Canada: Where our journeys begin and end.

The others, like Grace and Marge, Ken (who does woodwork as I do), and Ken B., the retired village policeman (who always has a smile and can make anyone laugh), have interesting stories to tell.

This little café in St. Marys is no different from many others all over America or Canada, and I have seen many of them in places like Hilton, N.Y., Biloxi, Miss., Grass Range, Mont., or Parker, Ariz.

Once we strolled in for coffee after recently having returned from Australia, and I offered a jar of Vegemite for everyone to try on toast. Vegemite is a dark brownish spread that looks like axle grease or road tar. It's a salty, thick paste made from a yeast extract.

Well, those townsfolk almost threw me bodily out of the café, with words to the effect of "Take that stuff out and don't bring it back!" They were kidding, of course, but they were serious about not trying any more Vegemite.

In the summer of 1997, Joyce and I met four Australians traveling on VIA Rail across British Columbia who were actually eating Vegemite during their lunch. They said they would not leave home without it. Something must be lacking in their diet!

XVIII. TOURING THE PACIFIC

In early September 1996, the "affable 60s-6," (Bill and Marge Jakes, Jack and Esther Robson, and Joyce and I) decided to go on a junket that would take us from Niagara Falls ARB to Alaska, Japan, Hawaii, California, and back to NFARB.

On Saturday, the day before we were to leave, Joyce and I had to travel back to Hilton, N.Y. to attend the 50th wedding anniversary celebration of my sister, Virginia ("Gin"), and her husband, Pete. Bill Jakes had made arrangements for us three couples to stay at the base that night, so when Joyce and I left my sister's party, we knew we were assured of a room when we arrived at the base late that night.

On Sunday morning I made arrangements to store my car at the long-term lot near the BOQ, and soon after the shuttle bus driver, a woman sergeant, was at the door to pick us up with our bags. It's only a short 10-minute walk to the Terminal Office, but with bags, it's a l-o-n-g walk (there is no AMC on that base). The 914th Air Wing is located there. They had flown us to the Azores and on to Ramstein, Germany in August 1995.

Armed with the knowledge of our previous trip (no box lunches available on board), this time we went well prepared with our lunches already made. The flights out of this base are so rare that there are no facilities on the base to provide meals even for crews, not to mention Space-A travelers.

Our C-130A departed around 11:30 a.m., and we set a northwesterly course that flew over Kitchener, Ontario, Thunder Bay on the north shore of Lake Superior, and the western part of Lake Winnipeg around 2:30 p.m. At 5 to 6 p.m. we were above the Canadian Rockies, and near 7 p.m. we approached the Gulf of Alaska shores. Arriving at 8 p.m., we landed at Elmendorf Air Force Base at Anchorage.

The six of us walked to the BOQ for Space-A lodging, and the next morning we ate breakfast at the Terminal, which was excellent.

Soon after, we were notified that the 914th boys could not fly us to Japan because they were making a stop at Shemya Island, out on the far chain of the Aleutians, near Attu. The base on Shemya is off-limits to civilians because there are no facilities available to nonmilitary types.

The sergeant at the AMC desk was very accommodating and told us to stand by. Shortly after, he found a flight from Seattle, the McChord Air Reserve Group, that was en route to Yokota Air Force Base near Tokyo, Japan. They had space available and were glad to take us on their C-141.

We arrived at Yokota Base on Wednesday, because we had skipped a day passing over the 180th meridian (International Date Line). It was their first time in Japan for the other five in our group, but I had been there two previous times during the Korean War. The scene was vastly different, as I knew it would be, from when I had been there before. Tall, modern skyscrapers had sprung up from the Tokyo streets, making the Imperial Palace look like a city park.

The people are also very different now, because a new generation has grown up since I was there (1950-52). The Japanese people have been in a state of denial since World War II. They have denied that they caused the war in the Pacific because, they say, the United States had cut them off from oil and rubber supplies in the Southeast Asia area. The official excuse is that they were forced to resort to aggression to gain what they needed. Their history has been rewritten to teach their children what they want the kids to believe. The war generation has never admitted to their children how they forced enemy soldiers and sailors to march for miles and miles with no water, and how their brave soldiers bayoneted the helpless unarmed Allied soldiers.

The six of us visited Tokyo, staying for five days at the New Sanno Hotel, operated by the U.S. military for the armed forces, both active and retired. We chartered a 50-passenger bus for a day's tour around the Mount Fuji area. I was hoping we would visit the Yamanaka Lake area and Shimoyoshida village, where I had been in 1950, but the tour covered an area on the other side of the mountain.

The young man who was our guide and driver spoke very good English and kept up a running commentary almost constantly the whole day.

On another day and night, we sat out Typhoon Violet at the hotel, listening as the wind and rain beat incessantly against the buildings and swept up the streets, bending the palm trees almost to the ground.

I had bought some china figurines that I thought were quite nice and would go with the Japanese motif in our master bedroom. A short time later, Joyce and I were browsing in the small Yokota Air Base bookstore (we visit every bookstore we see), and I spied a book that caught my attention. On the cover was a picture of a ship. The title of the book was *Bridge Across the Seas* (1995).

Scanning through it, I saw a picture of a ship inside. It was the *CGC Bering Strait!* I could not believe it! The authors were P. B. Innis and Walter D. Innis. The *Strait* was my old ship for over two years, 1950 through June '52. Tears welled up in my eyes as I called Joyce over to show her my find. I quickly bought the book and couldn't wait to read it back at our quarters that evening.

Finding that book was like finding a long-lost friend. The *Strait* had quite a war record, having served in the Navy from 1943 through '45. She was commissioned in the Coast Guard for over 25 years, and it was amazing that nothing had been written about the ship before.

According to *Bridge Across the Seas,* when the *Strait* was first commissioned, it seemed to be a "happy ship." I had sensed that when I first went aboard in March 1950, and I knew others felt that way, too. The *Bering Strait* just seemed to have a certain air about her, if that makes any sense. It was probably due to having a good crew and good officers, generally speaking. I don't recall hearing of anyone who wanted a transfer because he didn't like the ship.

After the six of us went to the Yokota Officers' Club for dinner, we separated and went to our respective accommodations for the evening. I dug into my newly found treasure and began to read about the *Strait's* exploits in World War II.

After a week's stay in Japan, we caught another flight of eight hours plus to Hickam Air Force Base in Hawaii. Bill and Jack had never been to Hawaii before, so the six of us toured Oahu, especially almost all of the military bases, along with Waikiki Beach.

One week in Hawaii was all too short, but we had to meet the 914th Air Group of Niagara Falls for our return to Travis Air Force Base in California. The next day we returned to Niagara Falls Air Reserve Base, safe and sound, and went our separate ways.

BIG ISLAND (HAWAII) AND SAMOA

At Christmas 1996, I decided to take Joyce to a bed-and-breakfast inn in Laguna Beach, California for the holiday. We stayed at Eilers' Inn, a cozy place with only 8 or 10 units. We checked in the day before Christmas, and wine and cheese were served, late in the afternoon, in the quaint fireplace room where all the entertaining is done.

We even had a room overlooking the ocean, if you looked over some of the roofs of buildings on some side streets. Our room had a gas fireplace, which we enjoyed into the late hours and again in the morning when we opened our gifts.

Going downstairs for the breakfast, we were greeted by five or six others, already gathered around the fireplace. The people were typical of those who stay at B&Bs, very friendly and congenial. One elderly lady from Lake Havasu City, Arizona said she takes this trip each year with two of her children and grandchildren. Her daughter and two of her grandchildren were there at the time.

On the day after Christmas, Joyce and I left and drove to San Diego to visit the city and its famous zoo. Leaving there in the late afternoon, we headed north and checked in at the Miramar Naval Airstation for the night.

Driving farther north, we checked in at March Air Reserve Base in Riverside for a possible Space-A flight to Hawaii. There was nothing available, so we drove back home.

A week later, checking on flights by telephone, I found one for that Saturday and another on Sunday. The secret is never to completely unpack your bags. You must be flexible, which is my adage.

On Saturday we found that all the space was going to be taken up by Acdutra personnel and their dependents. Driving to the BOQ (Bachelor

Officers' Quarters), we got a room for the night to await Sunday's outcome.

We arose bright and early Sunday morning and inquired at the AMC (Air Mobility Command) Terminal. Almost all the active duty personnel and their dependents had left the day before, so it was mainly all retired military, Category 6, waiting. I was the first man called to the desk, and I had papers and bags checked for both Joyce and me.

The aircraft was a KC-135 tanker that was escorting two F-105s across to Hawaii. When they started refueling over the Pacific, the load master sergeant called Joyce and me first to observe the refueling process at the tail. You go back and lie down on mattresses near the boom operator and see everything going on. The F-105 is only 50 feet and below, so you are looking right at the pilot. You observe the boom being maneuvered down and into the receptacle on the fuselage of the F-105. That is quite a thrill, and you are also looking straight down 35,000 feet to the sea below.

We arrived at Hickam AFB in about five hours and decided to check for lodging on the "Big Island." Within a half hour we had reservations for the lodge on the top of Kilauea, the most recent volcano. It's called KMC (Kilauea Military Camp), a large complex with many individual units, a large cafeteria serving three meals a day, entertainment at night, and a camp store.

The only unit available was the old fire house, where we stayed. Would you believe we had five bedrooms, a dining room, and a kitchen! There was a two-car garage, actually used by the two fire trucks at one time, where I could keep our rental car in either stall.

We rented an auto at the Hilo Airport and spent a week touring the coffee plantations and macadamia farms. All were very interesting, and we included a visit to Captain Cook's landing and the place where he was slain by the Sandwich Island natives. Driving back toward Kilauea Camp, we visited the southernmost tip of land in the United States. Unbeknownst to me at the time, my cousin's daughter lives on that barren, one-lane, pot-holed road that winds on down to the beach, called South Point.

Conversing with my cousin, Gail, at her mother's home in Needles, California, I learned how her daughter happens to live there and work at a bank in Kona. It seems that around her home she has roses, and Joyce and I had commented about the roses as we drove by. What a small world!

The week went by fast as we turned in the rental car at Hilo and enplaned for Honolulu. Taking the Mahalo Air flight back, Joyce and I began to think about where next to go to spend another week.

SAMOA

We arrived at Honolulu International, and after a fast taxi ride through the rain (yes, it rains frequently in the late afternoon), we checked the screen at the AMC Terminal. Pago Pago, American Samoa, was at the top of the board. We both took one glance and figured that was it. Our visas for Australia had expired, so we couldn't go there.

I got in line when the roll was called for Pago Pago and Australia. A retiree behind me asked, "You going to Australia?"

"No," I answered, "my wife and I are thinking of Pago Pago."

The fellow retorted, "What the hell do you want to go there for? There ain't nothin' there!"

"That's exactly why we want to go there," I said simply.

The AMC agent called me. "Where are you going?" he asked.

I replied immediately, "Pago Pago."

I was directed to take our bags to the counter to the right to check them and pay for our box lunches. After a short wait, maybe an hour or less, we were loaded onto the base shuttle and headed for the aircraft.

About six hours later we arrived in Pago Pago. We could feel the hot humid atmosphere at the small airport. We took our bags to a waiting taxi, and eight miles down the road we checked in at the famous Rainmaker Hotel. It's the only hotel on the island. Then I understood why people give you eye when you tell them you're going to Pago Pago.

The Rainmaker was very picturesque. I half expected to see Humphrey Bogart, Sydney Greenstreet, Peter Lorre, and Mary Astor in one of the open rooms as I walked by.

Joyce and I had dinner in the dining room the first night, and the food was excellent. The CD player was playing country/western music, *à la* Willie Nelson.

The next day we walked into town along the road because there are no sidewalks, and we visited some shops. We bought a few miscellaneous items, like lotion and toothpaste. I didn't see any T-shirts that caught my eye.

We talked with some of the people on the street, and they recommended the Captain's Cove, or something similar, for lunch. It seemed to be the place to go for many people there. A sandwich and a beer sufficed for both of us.

That afternoon we contacted a travel agency at the hotel and made arrangements to fly the next day to Western Samoa, an independent country since 1962.

On Wednesday, January 15, we took an island shuttle that gave us a scenic view of Pago Pago, just clearing the mountain peaks, as we departed and headed west for Upolu Island. An hour later, our 10-seat twin-engine turboprop circled another amazingly beautiful island. We landed at the gravel airstrip at Fagalii Airport.

"Talofa! Talofa!" we heard frequently as we went through Customs. We replied in kind, "Hello! Hello!" The Samoans are without a doubt the friendliest people in the world. No visa was required there. Australia is one of the very few countries that does require visas.

An old beat-up taxi took us to the far west side of Apia , the capital, where we checked in at the Kitano Tusitala Hotel. It is Japanese-owned and is designed with a the South Sea motif. For instance, the lobby is completely open on the sides, and blinds may be lowered if a rainstorm occurs.

The view was absolutely breathtaking as we gazed out of our unit (everything is on one floor) to see the steep mountains and the jungle in front. A farmer's pigs and his scrawny chickens running around created quite a scene. Those chickens would not have made even a very tasty chicken broth, to say nothing of a chicken dinner.

One of the most interesting sights was walking into the main area of Apia to see the fish market. The fish were all sizes and brightly colored, the likes of which I have never seen in the States.

On Friday, Joyce and I hired a minibus to take us on a tour of the island. One place we did not see was Vailiuma, the former home of Robert Louis Stevenson, the author of *Treasure Island* and other adventure novels.

Driving around the island, we had pointed out to us the taro plant growing, pineapple fields, and cocoanut and breadfruit trees. I have not had taro, the root of which is made into a paste, but someday I hope to taste it. A breadfruit is the size of a cocoanut or larger and weighs a pound or two. It is boiled and sliced and eaten like bread. I had tried it at the *fiafia (luau)* dinner at our hotel one night, but it cannot replace real baked bread.

With hopes of returning to Samoa in the future, I would certainly like to visit Vailiuma and the largest island, Savaii, often called the more beautiful of the two.

Joyce and I found the one and only McDonald's within 1,500 miles right there in Apia. We craved good old American coffee and a hamburger after eating fish and breadfruit for days.

Continuing around the countryside on the island drive, we observed the homes, called *fales* (thatched houses with open sides); some have steel roofing. The people sleep in the open on bed rolls that are rolled up and set aside during the day. If it storms, blinds are lowered to keep out the rain.

We decided to visit the Australian Embassy, located in one of the suites at the Aggie Grey Hotel. Joyce and I petitioned for renewed visas. It normally takes two or three days to get them, but we explained our urgency: we planned to be in Samoa only a day or two longer. The ambassador, a lady, delivered the visas to our hotel that very evening. How simple things are in small, less crowded places!

After a week in Samoa, we bade our *tofa* (good-bye) to the hotel clerks, waiters, and the bookkeeper as the cab arrived to take us back to the airstrip.

The cab driver, a very friendly fellow, told me he had been a Golden Gloves boxing champion back in the late 1930s. I did recall that Samoans were good boxers.

The terminal at Fagalii Airport is an old 12- by 15-foot shack with corrugated steel on the roof, and that is where you go through Customs, then check your bags outside. The terminal "waiting room" is a single wooden bench with no back, also outside!

Many of the Western Samoans fly to Pago Pago in American Samoa to buy food or clothings they cannot obtain on their home islands.

As an example of prices in Western Samoa, a cup of coffee at the McDonald's in Apia costs 1 Tala, 90 sene ($1.90) and a hamburger costs 2 Tala, 95 sene ($2.95).

The grocery store shelves are not that well stocked; there may be only five or six cans of each item, or maybe only one or two cans or packages each. Most foodstuffs have to be imported, usually from New Zealand. Fresh meat in Western Samoa especially comes from New Zealand.

There is a close relationship between Samoa and New Zealand. Considerable trade is carried on between the two countries. Vacationing in New Zealand is popular with Samoans who can afford it, and *vice versa,* New Zealanders love to go north for the winters. Many young Samoans get their higher education at New Zealand colleges.

Our flight was on time, and we departed that beautiful green emerald in the Pacific. Arriving in Pago Pago, we had about a four-hour wait for the USAF C-141. Leaving at 1700 hours (5 p.m.), we enjoyed the six-hour flight to Hickam AFB.

At Hickam we rented a car and went directly to the Submarine Base at Pearl Harbor for lodging.

The young sailor working as a desk clerk at the Officers' Quarters saw my ID card and asked, "Is a Coast Guard warrant officer about the same rank as a Navy captain?"

I laughed to myself. "Aaah, yes, it is *about* the same," I answered.

"That's good, sir," he continued. "I have a captain's suite for you on the third floor."

Joyce and I had to carry our own bags up to the third floor, but it was to a naval captain's suite with two richly appointed rooms.

We enjoyed Wednesday through Saturday, touring around the Honolulu area. On Saturday evening, a flight showed up on the base monitor for Sunday morning to March Air Reserve Base in California. The Hawaiian Air Guard was headed there, and there appeared to be enough seats available.

On Sunday morning, we showed up at 4 a.m. for the call-up, and at 0600 we departed Hawaii.

The C-141 was on time as we landed at 1 p.m. California time. I had contracted the flu and couldn't wait to get home. Joyce and I drove straight through to Lake Havasu City, Arizona, arriving at about 7 p.m.

XIX. BIG DIPPER TO SOUTHERN CROSS TO BIG DIPPER

One of the rapidly fading modes of travel is the cross-country passenger train. Our little village of St. Marys, Ontario is fortunate to have Canada's VIA Rail System serving the village. Two trains eastbound and two westbound pass through every day. The American AMTRAK System also passes through almost every day.

Our desire to see Canada cross-country by rail started in early July 1997.

The VIA System utilizes the Canadian National (CN) tracks most of the way from Toronto, passing through Parry Sound, Sudbury, Armstrong, Sioux Lookout, Winnipeg, Edmonton, and Jasper to Vancouver, British Columbia. We left the train at Jasper and boarded the VIA train *Skeena* for Prince George and finally Prince Rupert, BC, south of Alaska.

Accommodations on the train were adequate whether you took a coach or private compartment. The meals were well prepared and tasty. They were reasonably priced, and the service was very good.

After a day's rest in Prince Rupert, we took an Alaskan State Ferry for an overnight cruise to Ketchikan. I had last been there in 1949 on the *CGC Unalga*.

"What a change!" I remarked to Joyce. "I don't remember very much of the place, but I can see it's full of souvenir shops now!"

In 1948 or '49, the main industries and professions in Ketchikan were fishing, lumbering, and the well-known Creek Street enterprises. In 1997, I would say that tourism was the main industry by far. Joyce and I counted four cruise ships in port, not counting the ferry we were taking back to Prince Rupert.

The ferry was the *M/V Malaspina,* which the Canadian fishermen blockaded for three days, just after we disembarked at Prince Rupert. There was a problem of American fishermen encroaching on the area of Canadian fisheries, but the dispute was resolved between the two governments in a short time.

Taking a B.C. ferry down the inside passage of the Queen Charlotte Strait landed us at Port Hardy, where we visited our good friends, Ron and Nita Jack, in Port Alberni. They introduced us to the world of private bed-and-breakfast clubs, a fantastic form of overnight lodging almost anywhere in the world.

We toured the beautiful Olde English-styled city of Victoria and were introduced to two very nice bed-and-breakfast hosts, Marge and Des Pratt, who live north of Victoria. Marge kept us enthralled with descriptions from her new book, *Recollections of a Homesteader's Daughter,* and helped to inspire me in writing my story.

Des and Marge visited Lake Havasu City in February , and Joyce and I were very happy to host them for a couple of days. Marge brought us an autographed copy of her book, which we will always cherish.

50TH CLASS REUNION

Almost all the members of Hilton High School's Class of 1947 returned to Hilton for our 50th class reunion in September 1997.

We came to sing the school song:

> If to Hilton High we're loyal
> and the Red and White and Blue,
> We shall never fail to honor
> The school that made us true.

Our celebration was all too short; we had a big banquet and visited over small talk for three or four hours. We have had reunions every five years and, historically a close-knit group, we keep in fairly close contact with one another. There are a few who never attend or even acknowledge a contact over the years, but otherwise everyone was very congenial, and all seemed interested in one another's lives and health.

My old classmate Art and his wife Dottie now live in North Carolina on a golf course, where they are right at home. Art plays golf practically every day.

Bob, who had the Model A Ford 50 years ago, wishes he could find another one just like it.

Ken ("Stretch") and Annie, both former classmates, still live in Hilton and are still very much in love like the teenagers they once were.

Mary, the cute brunette I dated in high school, married Clayt, and they raised a family over the years. At our 50th reunion, I thought Mary was still the prettiest girl in the Class of 1947.

Some of us had lost our spouses over the years, but time has a way of healing our sorrows, and we all have to move on to other things.

The class has been very fortunate, for over the past 50 years we have lost only two classmates. I suppose we can expect to lose more at a faster rate in the future. We can only hope and pray and not dwell on what is to come.

SAVANNAH TO MELBOURNE

One trip Joyce and I hadn't taken up to 1997 was a freighter cruise. They are few and far between, but some are still available to serious-minded adventurers who do some searching.

I had known about them, having been in the Merchant Marine, and Joyce mentioned one day, "I would love to take a ship through the Panama Canal and someplace south."

"That really narrows it down a bit, dear!" I replied.

She had shown considerable interest since our wedding four years earlier in some of the nautical experiences I had had and in the places I'd sailed.

Our contact was with a German company, the Hamburg-Sud Lines, that sails between the East and West coasts of the U.S. and New Zealand and Australia.

A prerequisite, of course, was to go through the Panama Canal in the winter months, so we booked passage on the *Columbus America,* a 665-foot container ship sailing from Savannah, Georgia, headed for New Zealand and Australia.

We sailed on Thanksgiving Day 1997, but the ship, not being American, did not observe our holiday. Lunch consisted of boiled sausage, sauerkraut, boiled potatoes, and a banana!

On a freighter, there are no frills, no banquets, no orchestra on the mess deck, and no dancing until midnight.

Later friends asked us unbelievingly, "Well, what do you *do?*"almost wanting to hear us say, "Yes, there is a band every other night in the officers' salon," and "Oh, yes, we were served steak and lobster twice a week, and the waiters serenaded us at the tables."

Sorry! The food is adequate, but it cannot compare with that on American ships or on most other foreign ships. The German freighters are not known for their gourmet meals. As for entertainment, you had better take along six or eight books, at least, for a one-month trip (ours was 33 days to Melbourne). I read six books, and I wrote for three hours every morning, working on this book. There usually is a swimming pool aboard, and ours was 8 by 12 feet and up to 6 feet deep.

There were 10 passengers on the ship, all retired, mainly because retirees have all the time in the world to travel. Three widows told us they traveled extensively on freighters because they enjoyed going to exotic places and telling their friends that they "had been there."

There were two other couples besides Joyce and me, and each of us had double cabins. They were adequate with two bunks (some have double beds), a desk and a chair, a couch with a table and easy chair, a small refrigerator, and a private bathroom and shower. The rooms were cleaned daily by the stewards.

The 10th passenger had cases of beer brought aboard in port because he drank it after morning coffee and *ad infinitum.* The day for him was spent mostly reading, sleeping, and indulging—and quite frequently skipping meals so he could sleep it off.

The captain, first mate, and chief engineer were German. The six junior officers were for the most part Polish, and the crew (15-20) were Kiribati islanders (Gilbert Islands). All were top-notch professional sailors and willing to assist at all times.

Joyce and I enjoyed almost every minute of the cruise. She was extremely adept at navigating choppy seas and showed no inclination to be uncomfortable.

When aboard ship, I always feel 20 years younger (must be the salt air). Upon arising and cleaning up, I would go out on deck to scan the beautiful azure sky and the deep blue water. Breathing deeply of the fresh ocean air, I did calisthenics to loosen up, then joined Joyce as we went down to the officers' salon to greet our fellow passengers before breakfast.

It was alarming how fast the days went by on the freighter. At noon every day the ship's position would be marked on a world chart showing exactly where we were.

Occasionally another ship would be spotted on the horizon; it might be in sight for hours and then disappear. At times we would steam along for three or four days or longer before spotting another ship. The ocean, especially the Pacific, is an awfully large expanse of water to cross, about 10,000 nautical miles.

Leaving the ship at Melbourne, we journeyed by land to Sydney and from there to a small out-of-the-way village of 800 people, called Windsor, 45 miles to the west.

The entire village could be covered in 45 minutes, walking from the train station to the Windsor Motel at the other end of town. In between were quaint little stores and shops worth investigating, along with cozy little tearooms and a couple of pubs that served refreshments on a hot summer afternoon.

Even though our main purpose in spending a week at Windsor was to take an American Air Force plane back to Pago Pago and Hawaii, we fell in love with that little town and its surroundings. We met and made friends with some of the townspeople, such as Rev. Graham Whalen and Frank Elliott of St. Matthew's Anglican Church, where we attended the Sunday service. After the service, the ladies' group of the church served coffee and cookies on the side lawn, all of which was quite enjoyable, and everyone enjoyed small talk, especially about where we were from and what we had been doing. Someday I hope we can return there.

Arriving in Oahu, we spent two days at Waikiki and two days at a private bed-and-breakfast near Kaneohe Bay, on the north side of the island. After a week on Oahu, we found a C-141 flight to McClellan Field, near Sacramento, from which we drove the 600 miles to home in Arizona.

December 1997: Joyce and I on our freighter cruise. Behind us is the Bridge of the Americas across the Panama Canal, linking South America (on the left) to North America (on the right).

ANCHORAGE, ALASKA

A short, spur-of-the-moment journey to Alaska came upon us in the middle of June 1998.

The 914th ARW of Niagara Falls Air Reserve Base was flying out on a Monday to Elmendorf AFB in Anchorage and returning on Friday. They had space available for 10 to 15 passengers.

Leaving that Monday morning, I was pleasantly surprised to see a good friend of mine, Sgt. Bill Lawsen, a crew chief on the flight.

Bill and I had been friends for years because we both were members of the National Warplane Museum in New York State. He was a mechanic volunteering at the museum, and I worked at restoring various planes, like the B-17, "Fuddy Duddy," a PBY, and a P-47 that was on loan to us.

I believe Bill was on the flight crew at some of the air shows when I was flying the Stearman.

He was also on the same flight the six of us took in September 1996 when we flew from NFARB to Alaska and eventually returned from Hawaii to Niagara Falls.

Joyce and I enjoyed the four days we spent in Alaska. We made use of our B&B Club membership while staying there.

Renting a car, we saw much wildlife and breathtaking scenery between Seward and Palmer. Stopping along the roadside, Joyce was able to catch a spectacular close-up of a mountain sheep not more than 40 or 50 feet away. An hour later we were able to snap a scene with a cow moose not more than 100 feet away.

When we told our daily adventures to our B&B hosts, Keith exclaimed, "Do you realize that some natives around here never see scenes like that in a lifetime?"

"Yes," we said, "we were very fortunate. We realize that." We simply happened to be in the right spot at the right time.

The next day, we travelled north to Palmer, to visit a musk oxen farm (they are not native to Alaska) and to a Grey Wolf Farm, which proved to be very fascinating. The wolves were tied up on long chains but being well fed, they appeared quite docile. The trainer had me hold a small biscuit in my hand for one wolf to jump for it. Joyce volunteered to hold another small biscuit in HER TEETH as another wolf took it from her. The canines all had names, such as "Digger," as he likes to dig holes, or "Slinky," as she likes to slink around with her head low all the time.

Friday morning our flight left exactly on time from Elmendorf Air Force Base and eleven hours later we touched down on the NFARB runway.

Returning to our summer home in St. Marys, Ont., we quickly got back into the swing of things again; Joyce tending to her flowers around the house and around the fish pond in the back and I had to catch up on the weeds in our garden and the rapidly growing lawn.

We enjoy our lily pond in the back with the fantails, chibunkans and gold fish living there along with our bull and spotted leopard frogs lazing around.

It was time for my monthly trim from Ron the barber in St. Marys, the other day. He conducts his "tonsorial" business in the basement of his home where there is never a waiting line because he takes customers by appointment. I have found that barbers, over the length and breadth of this globe, are pretty much the same, that is, they are for the most part, great conversationalists.

Ron was telling me, "You won't believe this. I had this one fellow, an occasional customer, come in the other day and I asked him how he wanted his hair cut."

He said, "Well, short on the left side and leave it long over the right ear. Trim the right eyebrow and leave the left one alone."

I said, "Huh? Why is that?"

He replied, "Well,---- cut it the same way, like YOU CUT IT BEFORE!"

"Then the fellow burst out laughing and said he was just kidding. You never know what to expect."

Hal ran a barbershop in the village where I lived and was known as quite a conversationalist. There was an old story that went around, years ago, when one of the local men came in for a haircut and got Hal's chair. Hal asked, "How do you want your hair cut, Jess?"

Jess simply said, "In COMPLETE SILENCE, Hal!

More than once, there may be 4 or 5 customers waiting for haircuts and a couple of them in the very back chairs might be talking about fishing and Hal's ears would perk up. His scissors would gradually slow down as he would cock an ear for the conversation. Then the snip - snip - snip of the scissors would grind to a halt. Listening for an opening, he would interject a word or two into the story.

Before you knew it, he had completely left his customer in the chair and was back near the fellows that were conversing and joined in the conversation himself, as he waved his scissors and comb in the air.

Sometimes, it took an hour or longer to get a haircut, depending on whether there was an interesting story or not.

My friend, Jim's grandfather, Bert, owned and operated a barbershop for many, many years in Hilton. After Bert died in 1952, the shop was closed for some time, then a fellow by the name of Vernon came out of retirement in Rochester and reopened the shop. Vernon had owned and operated an 8-chair hair styling salon in Rochester for many years and after being retired for some time, he wanted something to do.

He was a very interesting man and wasn't adverse to imbibing every so often during working hours, either.

More than once, I had heard that Vernon would be cutting someone's hair and he would suddenly excuse himself, in the middle of a trim, run across Main Street, down one or two hookers, for courage, then return back to his customer. One friend said that after waiting 10 minutes, for Vernon to return, he left and never went back to him again.

Another day, a fellow came in to Vernon's Shop and sat down to wait his turn. Shortly, the man inquired of Vernon, if he had a toilet there.

Vernon said, "Yes, just go out the rear door, turn left, then take the first right."

The man was dressed quite well in a pair of slacks and a long sleeve white shirt with the cuffs turned up. Seconds later there was a "bang - c-r-a-s-h, rumble - rumble" then - silence. A couple of minutes later this same fellow came back in the front door of the shop.

Vernon, obviously quite shocked asked, "My GOD, man, what happened to you?"

This chap had scrapes and bruises on his arms and face. His hair was all disheveled and the white shirt sleeves were blackened and ripped.

He said, "What are you trying to do? Kill me? You told me to go through that door, turn right, then take the first left!"

Vernon said, "Oh, NO, NO! I told you to go out the door, turn LEFT, then TAKE THE FIRST RIGHT!"

Seems that this poor soul misunderstood the directions and as he turned RIGHT and then LEFT - he stepped into a darkened stairway and went tumbling down into the basement and landed in the coal bin.

When he came back upstairs, he even turned wrong and went outside, then found his way back into the front of the shop.

A friend of mine, Ellwood, happened to be sitting in the chair, at the time, and witnessed the whole event.

Ellwood got his haircut and LEFT!

The poor unfortunate chap, did NOT get his haircut and LEFT!

Vernon cut hair for a short time, then closed up shop permanently and HE LEFT!

XX. FAMILY GET-TOGETHER: PAST AND FUTURE

Attending a family wedding in August afforded a chance for the entire family to be together for the first time in many years.

Sherryl is married to George, and they have three children: Michael, Karen, and Laura. Now all three children are grown and married with families of their own.

Richard is married to Kathy, and they have two sons, Brian and Aaron. Bonny is married to Richard, and they have a daughter, Laurie, and a son, Scott. Now both Laurie and Scott are married with families.

Deborah was there with Dorothy and her husband Chris and their family: Chante, Chelsea, and C. Tanner. Jon, Dot's son from a previous marriage, was also there. Michelle, Dot's eldest daughter, also from the previous marriage, was unable to attend because she lives in Oklahoma City, Oklahoma with her husband Jason and son Jason Jr. Little Jason is my great-grandson!

Dan and his wife Beth were there with their two sons, Jimmy and Ricky.

Jim and Rick cornered me for a few minutes to inquire, "Grandpa, can you remember all the cars you ever owned?"

Gosh, I had to think about that for a while.

"Well," I began, "in 1952 I bought my first car, a maroon 1950 Ford, two-door Custom. It was light and fast and had overdrive transmission."

Then I told them about my 1953 Chevrolet Bel Air. It was economical but had no power on pickup. The 1956 Chevrolet Nomad wagon was a sharp car, and it became a classic, but mine had more miles on it from being pushed or towed than from being driven. Replacing fuel pumps every few months became a ritual.

A 1957 Ford Tudor we had (1961-65) was a good runner, but it rusted badly around the front headlamps. We used it for a few trips back and forth from Hilton to Biloxi, Mississippi, where I was transferred by General Dynamics Corp.

Our 1963 Oldsmobile Super 88 was an excellent car that we kept for four years; then the '67 Oldsmobile Delta 88 was odd. It handled weirdly for some unknown reason.

Then I ordered a new 1972 Ford Galaxie that was excellent in every way. That was followed by a '76 Mustang Il Ghia that had to be specially made with a larger trunk for my golf clubs. That was a good car, except that the headlamps burned out every three months and had to be replaced. The car was actually a little too small for me.

My next vehicle was a 1977 Pontiac Grand Prix, an excellent car, then an '83 Grand Prix that I had for only a few months before someone rear-ended me and totaled the car. So I bought an '84 Grand Prix exactly like it, and that was an excellent car.

Grand Prix dropped its annual models in 1987, so I acquired a showroom car from Hallman Chevrolet, a limited edition of an '87 Monte Carlo Super Sport/Aerocoupe. Dale Earnhardt, the NASCAR driver, drove a model just like it for years. This SS was a classic, but it had stiff suspension for riding, and it didn't have air conditioning.

When I retired from GMC in June 1991, I bought a '91 Buick Regal through the Employee Purchase Plan. The Regal was a super car all the way.

Now I still have a 1996 Buick Park Avenue, which is probably the best car I've ever owned.

For sports cars, I had a 1959 Karmann Ghia for two years when Dan was in high school (1975-76). Next was a 1960 Corvette, bought in 1980 as a basket case and restored to its original shape. It was a great classic and a show car that won a few trophies.

In 1982 I had a chance to buy a 1957 Corvette, which was my favorite. Later, with an '83 Grand Prix, a '72 Triumph, and two 'Vettes, I was crowded for space, so I sorrowfully sold the '57 'Vette because it was extremely hard to find parts for it.

Finding a 1968 Austin Healy Mk3-3000 locally was almost too good to be true. I picked that up and sold the Triumph because the Healy was, to me, the true sports car.

By that time I had my Starduster II biplane, so by 1991 I had sold all my cars before retiring from General Motors.

After living in Arizona for a couple of years, I got itchy for something sporty, so I bought a 1978 MG Midget and later found a '76 El Camino in excellent shape. The pickup was obviously a California car (no rust), so we plan to enjoy it for a long time in the Arizona desert.

After all that, Ricky said, "Wow! You must be pretty old to own all those cars, Grandpa!"

"Hey," I retorted, "if you live long enough, you'll get old." Actually, I feel pretty young.

SAILING

Dan said, "Jim and Rick, why don't you ask Grandpa where he has sailed over the years? You knew about his flying, but you never knew much about his sailing on ships."

Jim gathered his three cousins, Chante, Chelsea, and Jillian, Gary's daughter from Canada, to join in.

Chante, very inquisitive, asked, "Were you on big boats like we have on Lake Ontario?"

"Some of those boats on Lake Ontario are pretty big," I said. "I've been on smaller ones and probably some larger ones. Some Coast Guard ships are about as long as a football field, 260 to 365 feet. The Merchant Marine ships were 460 to 665 feet long."

I told them that I had sailed on ships in the Pacific, Atlantic, and Indian Oceans, on the Bering, Mediterranean, Tasman, Coral, Sagami, and Arabian Seas, and on the Gulfs of Mexico, Alaska, Panama, Persian, Aden, Oman, and Suez.

"None of them," I added, "held any more adventure and very little more excitement than my sailing down Salmon Creek on that raft with my boyhood chum and my dog Lucky, some 60 years ago."

August 1998: Most, but not all, of the Walters family met for a reunion in Hilton, N.Y.

After leaving the family get-together, Joyce and I stopped, as we always do, at the Niagara Falls Air Reserve to check on flight possibilities for the future. We are planning a little trip to Germany and England.

in the fall to look up some family roots. My mother's side of the family has been traced to back to the early 1500s around Braintree, Essex County, England. My father's side goes back to the area around Wurzberg, Germany.

Coming up on our agenda next winter will be a revisit to the Samoas and Australia. Our dear friends, Bill and Marge Jakes, who winter in Lakeland, Florida, are thinking seriously of joining us for the exciting, stimulating, sensational journey to the South Seas. I, for one, look forward to the return to Pago Pago and Western Samoa, where Joyce and I have formed good friendships. A return to Australia is always an electrifying thought. This time we have in mind Alice Springs, the Outback, quaint little Windsor, and bustling Sydney and Melbounre.

That's 30!

The best advice I have for young people is: Don't wait to enjoy life until it's too late.

Children should enjoy play and not be too regulated or regimented by adults. For instance, Little League Baseball puts too much emphasis on winning and too much pressure on some little folks. Competitive beauty pageants and figure skating competitions can also be too demanding on some children. Let children play their own games until they reach 14 or 15.

Enjoy life as you live every day. That does not mean that you need money to enjoy things. There are many things that require money for enjoyment, but the best things in life are free.

Stop to smell the roses every day! Enjoy the trees and the birds, the flora and fauna, and enjoy people.

When I was young in the U.S. Coast Guard, on the *Unalga* in the Aleutian Islands, we didn't see a tree for five or six months. When our ship returned to the Straits of Juan de Fuca, before entering Seattle harbor, before we spotted land, there was the smell of evergreen in the air. One of the most captivating sights I ever witnessed was those evergreens as we drew within sight. They very simply signified life and beauty here on Earth to me.

TREES*

I think that I shall never see
A poem lovely as a tree.

A tree whose hungry mouth is prest
Against the earth's sweet flowing breast;

A tree that looks at God all day,
And lifts her leafy arms to pray;

---

*By Joyce Kilmer.

A tree that may in Summer wear
A nest of robins in her hair;

Upon whose bosom snow has lain;
Who intimately lives with rain.

Poems are made by fools like me,
But only God can make a tree.

I would also say: Dare to be different! I believe children should be encouraged to "shoot for the moon!" Eighty percent of us would probably never make it, but give it your best shot. Ideals and ideas change over the years, but along the way you will have seized the opportunity.

Do not allow yourself to be led like sheep. Stand up and speak out for what you believe in, when in your heart you know what is right.

Some men only dream, while others make their dreams come true.

That's really 30!